BIBLE STORY
Coloring Pages

Illustrated by Chizuko Yasuda

Gospel Light

How to make clean copies from this book

You may make copies of portions of this book with a clean conscience if:

• you (or someone in your organization) are the original purchaser;

• you are using the copies you make for a noncommercial purpose (such as teaching or promoting your ministry) within your church or organization;

• you follow the instructions provided in this book.

However, it is ILLEGAL for you to make copies if:

• you are using the material to promote, advertise or sell a product or service other than for ministry fund-raising;

• you are using the material in or on a product for sale;

• you or your organization are not the original purchaser of this book.

By following these guidelines you help us keep our products affordable.

Thank you, Gospel Light

Gospel Light

Editorial Staff

Editor, Deborah Barber • **Contributing Editor**, Linda Mattia • **Designer**, Carolyn Thomas • **Illustrator**, Chizuko Yasuda

Publisher, William T. Greig • **Senior Consulting Publisher**, Dr. Elmer L. Towns • **Publisher, Research, Planning and Development**, Billie Baptiste • **Senior Editor**, Lynnette Pennings • **Senior Consulting Editors**, Dr. Gary S. Greig, Wesley Haystead, M.S.Ed. • **Editor, Theological and Biblical Issues**, Bayard Taylor, M.Div.

©1997 Gospel Light, Ventura, CA 93006. All rights reserved. Printed in U.S.A.

Great Ways to Use These Pages:

▲ **Review for Early Arrivals:** Photocopy pictures of Bible stories you have recently talked about. Early arrivals can have a choice of pictures to color, giving you opportunities to talk with children about what they recall about that story. Also, have copies available for transition times or for children who finish an activity ahead of others.

▲ **Story-Telling Tool:** Photocopy the appropriate coloring page to use as a visual aid during story telling time. As you tell story, color in parts of the picture to keep children's interest and to help them focus on the part of the story you are telling. For even more fun, try making transparencies and coloring them on an overhead projector as you tell the story!

▲ **Story Review:** Photocopy a coloring page for each student. Ask questions to review the story as children color.

▲ **Coloring Game:** After you've told the Bible story, place a variety of colored markers on the table. Distribute copies of picture from Bible story. Volunteers tell one part of the Bible story. Then each child chooses a marker and uses it to color one part of his or her page. When finished, children put markers down and tell another part of the Bible story. Children then choose another marker and color another part of the page. Repeat process until pages (and story!) are completed.

▲ **Concentration Game:** Reduce and photocopy a set of two pictures of each story you have talked about. Invite volunteers to color each set alike. Then place pictures facedown on the floor. Children take turns

turning over two pictures at a time, trying to find two matching pictures. Play continues until all picture sets have been paired.

▲ **Guessing Game:** Color (or invite volunteers to color) ten or more pictures that you have talked about. Display completed pictures. Give three clues for a story. Children try to guess which story you are describing.   Examples of clues might be, "I'm thinking of a happy night." "I'm thinking of some good news that some people heard." "I'm thinking of a very special baby."

▲ **Individual Coloring Books:** Photocopy several coloring pages for each child in your class. Fold 11x17-inch (27.5x42.5-cm) construction paper over pages and staple to make individual coloring books.

 ▲ **Bible Story Puzzle:** Color, then paste completed coloring page onto poster board. Cover with clear adhesive paper and cut into puzzle pieces. Place puzzle pieces in a resealable sandwich bag and label. Offer puzzles during transition times or to early arrivals.

▲ **Great Gift:** Give to your children as a great substitute for secular coloring books.

▲ **Parent Involvement:** Send two copies of uncolored coloring pages and stories home with children (be sure to duplex so stories are on the back of page). Include a note to encourage parents to read Bible stories and color pages with their children.

▲ **Felt Board Figures:** Glue colored coloring page to poster board. Cut out main characters. Glue strips of felt to the backs of characters and use with felt board.

▲ **Puppets:** Color main characters on coloring page and glue to poster board. Cut out and glue characters to craft sticks. Give to children to use as stick puppets.

Contents: Old Testament

Contents: New Testament

God creates the world.

Genesis 1:1—2:25

God creates the world.

Genesis 1:1—2:25

In the beginning, before anything was anything, God made the heavens and the earth. He just said, "Let there be light," and there was light! Then God made the sky and the land and the oceans. God made the plants and the sun, moon and stars. He liked what He made. It was very good!

Then God said, "Let the sky be filled with birds that fly." And it was. He said, "Let the waters be filled with all sorts of creatures." Then there were fish, dolphins, jellyfish, and many other creatures in the water. Next, God made every kind of animal. When God saw all the creatures that He made, He said that they were very good.

Then God did something even more special! He took some dirt and formed it into a man. Then God breathed into the man and he became alive. Next, God made a woman. They were the first people—people like you and me. They were named Adam and Eve. God loved Adam and Eve. Everything God made was very good.

Adam and Eve disobey God.

Genesis 3:1-24

Adam and Eve disobey God.

Genesis 3:1-24

Adam and Eve lived in a wonderful garden. There were trees and plants with good food like apples, bananas, grapes and watermelon. There were flowers and trees and plants that were beautiful to look at.

In the middle of the garden was a tree called the tree of the knowledge of good and evil. God told Adam and Eve they could eat anything in the whole garden except the fruit that was growing on that one tree.

One day, a serpent talked to Eve and told her to eat the forbidden fruit. "If you eat some of that fruit, you would know things you didn't know before," the snake said. "You would be like God."

Eve listened to the serpent. She ate some of the fruit from the tree that God said not to eat from. Adam ate some, too. God was very sad that they had disobeyed Him. Adam and Eve had to leave the beautiful garden, but God still loved them very much.

Noah builds an ark.

Genesis 6:1-22

Noah builds an ark.

Genesis 6:1-22

Adam and Eve had children, and their children had children. After a while there were many people everywhere. But they did not love and obey God. They hurt other people and did not follow God's rules. God was sorry He had made them.

There was one person left who loved God. His name was Noah. Noah did what was right. God told Noah that He was going to send a flood to cover the whole world.

"Make a big boat," God told Noah. The boat was called an ark. Noah and his family would be safe in the ark when the flood came.

Noah and his family obeyed God. They worked hard to build the ark. They worked hard to gather lots of food. After a long time, the ark was ready. Noah and his family were ready.

God keeps Noah and the animals safe.
Genesis 7:1-24

God keeps Noah
and the animals safe.

Genesis 7:1-24

God was going to send a flood. Noah built a big boat called an ark. Now God wanted Noah to fill the ark with some of every kind of animal. There were two elephants, two monkeys, two bears and two pigs. There were many, many more kinds of animals, too. Noah and his family helped all the animals on the ark. It must have been hard work!

Finally all the animals were inside the ark. The sky grew dark and cloudy. Soon Noah's family heard rain falling on the roof. It wasn't long before the ark was floating on the water. The ark rocked back and forth. It rained and rained and rained for forty days.

Noah's family probably heard lots of strange noises! It must have been scary at first. But God kept everyone inside the ark safe. While they waited in the ark, the whole world was covered with water. Even the tops of the tall, tall mountains were covered. Everything that was not in the ark was destroyed.

God makes a promise. Genesis 8:1—9:17

God makes a promise.

Genesis 8:1—9:17

The earth was covered with water for a long time. Finally, the water went away enough for the bottom of the ark to rest on a mountain. The earth began to dry up.

Noah and his family and all the animals stayed on the ark for many days. When the earth was dry enough, God told Noah to come out of the ark. Noah's family must have been so excited! The animals must have been very excited, too. It had been a long time since they had been able to run and climb and leap on dry ground.

After he let all the animals out of the ark, Noah built an altar, a special place to worship God. Noah thanked God for keeping his family safe during the flood.

God was happy to hear Noah praying. He promised Noah that He would never again destroy all living things with a flood. God put a rainbow in the sky to remind everyone of His promise.

Abram travels to a new home.

Genesis 12:1-9

Abram travels to a new home.

Genesis 12:1-9

God loved Abram. God told Abram to leave his home and go to a new land. God promised to make Abram the leader of a great nation.

Abram obeyed God. He and his wife and his nephew, Lot, left their home. They took all their animals and their helpers with them. They walked for many, many days.

After days and days of walking, Abram and his family arrived in the new land. God told him that He was going to give the land to Abram's children. Abram worshiped God. Abram trusted God. Abram believed that God would keep His promises.

Isaac is born.

Genesis 15:1-6; 17:1-8; 18:1-15; 21:1-7

Isaac is born.

Genesis 15:1-6; 17:1-8; 18:1-15; 21:1-7

God gave a special promise to Abram. He promised to give Abram and his wife a son. As a reminder of His promise, God changed Abram's name to Abraham. Abraham means "father of many." Abraham and his wife, Sarah, waited many years but they still did not have a child. Abraham still did not stop believing God's promise.

Abraham and Sarah grew very old, older than most grandparents. One day some angels visited Abraham. "Next year Sarah will have a son," the visitors said.

Sarah was sitting in her tent listening to Abraham and the visitors. When she heard the angels' words, she started to laugh. She and Abraham were almost one hundred years old! She knew that no one her age ever had a baby. She was just too old! The visitors knew that she laughed. They said, "Is anything too hard for God?"

God kept His promise to Abraham and Sarah. The next year, Sarah had a baby boy just as God had said. Abraham and Sarah named him Isaac.

Abraham's servant finds a wife for Isaac.

Genesis 24:1-67

Abraham's servant finds a wife for Isaac.

Genesis 24:1-67

Isaac grew up and soon it was time for him to get married. Abraham talked to his servant. "Promise me that you will find a wife for my son Isaac." His servant promised to do his best.

The servant loaded many gifts on some camels. He traveled through the hot, dry desert to the land where Abraham used to live. Abraham's servant stopped by the well in a town. The servant asked God to show him who Isaac's new wife would be.

While he was praying, a beautiful woman named Rebekah came to the well. Abraham's servant asked her for some water. She gave him a drink and then said, "I'll give water to your camels, also." Rebekah worked hard pouring water into the watering trough until the thirsty camels had enough water. Abraham's servant knew that this kind person was the one God wanted to be Isaac's wife.

Abraham's servant was glad that God answered his prayer. Rebekah was happy to be Isaac's wife.

Isaac chooses not to fight.

Genesis 26:12-33

Isaac chooses not to fight.

Genesis 26:12-33

Isaac needed to dig a well so his family and his helpers and his animals could have good water to drink. Isaac's helpers worked hard digging deep into the ground. Then, water began to fill up the hole!

Everyone was happy except Isaac's neighbors. They shouted, "That well is ours!" Isaac did not want to fight with his neighbors. So Isaac let them have the well. Isaac moved on to another place. He told his helpers to dig another well.

The helpers worked hard again. Soon water began to fill up the hole. But then Isaac's neighbors came again. "That well is ours!" they shouted.

Isaac still wanted to be kind to his neighbors. So Isaac moved to another place again. And he told his helpers to dig another well. That night God said to Isaac, "Do not be afraid, Isaac. I will always be with you."

Isaac's neighbors came again. They said, "We will not fight with you any more." Isaac was very happy! Isaac was glad God had helped him to be kind.

Jacob tricks Esau.
Genesis 25:19-34; 27:1-41

Jacob tricks Esau.

Genesis 25:19-34; 27:1-41

Jacob and Esau were twin brothers. Esau was born first, so he was supposed to be the next leader of the family. Esau loved to hunt and be outside. Jacob was quiet and stayed at home.

One day Jacob was cooking some stew. Esau came home from hunting and he was very hungry. "Give me some of your stew," he said.

"I'll give you some stew if you give me the right to lead the family when our father dies," Jacob answered. So Esau gave his birthright to Jacob. Esau wanted the stew more than he wanted to be his family's leader.

Another time, Jacob dressed up like Esau. Jacob put some goat's skin on his arms and chest so he would feel hairy like Esau. Jacob put on some of Esau's clothes so he would smell sweaty like Esau. (They didn't wash their clothes very often back then!) Jacob talked to Isaac, but because Isaac was almost blind Isaac thought Jacob was really Esau! Isaac prayed for Jacob, and made promises to him, promises he had meant to make to Esau. When Esau found out about Jacob's trick he was very angry.

Jacob has a dream.

Genesis 27:41-45; 28:10-22

Jacob has a dream.

Genesis 27:41-45; 28:10-22

Jacob tricked his father and his brother, Esau. Esau was so angry he wanted to hurt Jacob. Jacob was afraid. Jacob's mother told Jacob to run away to his uncle's house, where he would be safe.

So Jacob walked all day. When it was night, he stopped to sleep. He laid down on the ground and put a stone under his head for a pillow.

While Jacob slept, he had a dream. He saw a stairway reaching up to heaven. He saw angels on the stairway. They were going up and down. At the top of the stairway, Jacob saw God!

God told Jacob that He would make Jacob's family into a great nation. God promised to be with Jacob and to take care of him. Jacob woke up and promised to obey God.

Jacob goes home.

Genesis 31:1—33:20

Jacob goes home.

Genesis 31:1—33:20

Jacob lived with his uncle for a long time. Jacob had many sheep, goats, donkeys and camels. Jacob got married and had many children. After many years, God told Jacob it was time to go back home to the land where he used to live.

Jacob took his wives and children and all his animals and servants. They left Jacob's uncle's farm and traveled to the place God told them to go. But Jacob was afraid to go home.

Jacob was afraid because when he was younger, he had cheated his brother, Esau. Esau had been very angry and had wanted to hurt Jacob. Jacob was afraid that Esau would still want to hurt him. Jacob was afraid that Esau might still be so angry that he would hurt Jacob's family. So Jacob asked God to help him. And God took care of Jacob. Esau forgave Jacob and was kind to him.

Joseph's brothers sell him.

Genesis 37:2-36

Joseph's brothers sell him.

Genesis 37:2-36

Joseph's father, Jacob, loved Joseph more than any of Joseph's other brothers. Jacob gave Joseph a special coat to show that Joseph was his favorite son. Joseph had dreams about being in charge of the family even though he was one of the youngest brothers. Joseph's brothers thought that Joseph was always bragging.

One day Jacob sent Joseph to check on his brothers while they were taking care of the sheep. Joseph walked a long time. Finally he found his brothers and the sheep.

When his brothers saw Joseph coming, they decided to get rid of Joseph by throwing him into a dry well. While the brothers were eating lunch, they saw a caravan headed for Egypt. They pulled Joseph out of the well and sold him as a slave to the people in the caravan.

Then Joseph's brothers took Joseph's coat and tore it up so that it looked like a wild animal had attacked him. They told their father, Jacob, that they found Joseph's coat in a field. Jacob was sad because he thought that Joseph was dead.

Joseph helps Pharaoh.

Genesis 39:1—41:49

Joseph helps Pharaoh.

Genesis 39:1—41:49

Joseph was sold as a slave to an Egyptian official. Later, Joseph was put in prison because the official's wife told a lie about him. But God took care of Joseph. God helped Joseph talk to Pharaoh (the king)!

Joseph warned Pharaoh that there would be seven years when lots of food would grow in the fields and then seven years when no food would grow in the fields. "You need to put someone in charge of collecting food. Then when there is no food growing in the fields, there will still be food for everyone to eat."

Pharaoh liked what Joseph said. He put Joseph in charge of collecting food. Pharaoh gave Joseph a ring and some fancy new clothes. He even gave Joseph a chariot to ride in!

Joseph traveled all over Egypt and made sure that there would be plenty of food to eat for everyone. God helped Joseph take care of all the people.

Joseph forgives his brothers.

Genesis 42:1—45:28

Joseph forgives his brothers.

Genesis 42:1—45:28

Jacob's family didn't have any food. Jacob heard that there was food to buy in Egypt. He sent Joseph's brothers there to buy food. Joseph's brothers didn't know that God had helped Joseph become an important ruler in Egypt.

When Joseph's brothers got to Egypt, they asked to buy food. They did not know they were talking to Joseph. It had been a long time since they had seen Joseph. Joseph had grown up. Now he dressed and talked like an Egyptian.

Joseph pretended that he did not know his brothers. He asked them about their family. Joseph tested them to see if they were sorry for being mean to him. Then Joseph told his brothers who he was, and he forgave them. Joseph invited them all to come and live near him in Egypt. Joseph was glad to be with his family again.

The people of Israel are slaves in Egypt.

Exodus 1:1-22

The people of Israel are slaves in Egypt.

Exodus 1:1-22

Joseph's brothers and father and all their families moved to Egypt. They lived there for many years. They had children and their children had children. They were called Israelites. Soon there were many Israelites in Egypt.

There was a new king in Egypt now. This Pharaoh didn't know the good things that Joseph had done for his country. He was afraid of the Israelites because there were so many of them. He thought they might take over the country. The new Pharaoh made the Israelites his slaves. That means he made them work hard and didn't pay them.

Even though the Egyptians treated the Israelite slaves very badly, God had a plan to help the Israelites.

God protects baby Moses.

Exodus 2:1-10

God protects baby Moses.

Exodus 2:1-10

Pharaoh was afraid of the Israelites. There were many Israelites in Egypt. Pharaoh thought there were too many Israelites. Pharaoh planned to stop them by hurting all the Israelite baby boys.

But one mother hid her baby boy from the Egyptian soldiers. When she couldn't hide him anymore, she made a basket that would float. She put the baby in the basket and carefully put it on the river. The baby's big sister, Miriam, hid nearby to watch what would happen.

Pharaoh's daughter came to the river with her servants to take a bath. The princess saw the basket and sent one of her servants to get it. When she opened the basket, the baby was crying. The Princess felt sorry for him.

Miriam ran up to the princess and said, "Shall I go and get someone to take care of this baby for you?" The princess said yes. So Miriam brought her mother to the princess. The princess told the mother to take care of the baby. Later the princess named the baby Moses. When Moses grew up, he lived with the princess, right in the Pharaoh's palace!

God talks to Moses.

Exodus 3:1—4:17

Bible Story Coloring Pages • 43

God talks to Moses.

Exodus 3:1—4:17

Grown-up Moses went to live in the desert. He took care of some sheep. One day he saw something strange. A bush was on fire, but it did not burn up! Moses walked near the bush to see why it didn't burn up.

God spoke to Moses from the bush. He said, "Moses, take off your shoes. This is a holy place." Moses knew it was God talking. God said, "Moses, tell Pharaoh to let my people go free." God did not want the Israelites to be slaves anymore. God wanted Moses to be the leader of the Israelites.

Moses was afraid. He was afraid that Pharaoh would not listen to him. Moses was afraid that the Israelites would not listen to him.

God told Moses that He would help Moses do what God wanted. Moses would even be able to do miracles. Then Pharaoh would do what God wanted. But Moses was still afraid. So God told Moses that Moses' brother Aaron would help him. Finally, Moses was ready to go talk to Pharaoh.

Moses says,
"Let my
people go."
Exodus 5:1—12:32

Moses says, "Let my people go."

Exodus 5:1—12:32

Moses went to Pharaoh. "God said to let His people go," Moses said. Pharaoh did not listen. Pharaoh did not care about what God said. Instead, he made the Israelites work even harder!

Moses went to see Pharaoh again. He told Pharaoh, "God is going to send terrible troubles on Egypt if you do not let the Israelites go." Pharaoh didn't care. He said no again!

God made terrible things happen in Egypt because Pharaoh would not listen to God. The troubles got worse and worse. Frogs came out of the river and got into everything. There were bugs everywhere. All the animals in the fields died. People got terrible sores and all the plants were destroyed. But Pharaoh still refused to let the Israelites go.

Finally, even Pharaoh's own son died. Then Pharaoh knew that God was powerful. Pharaoh told Moses and the Israelites to leave.

Moses leads the people out of Egypt.

Exodus 12:33-39; 13:17-22

Moses leads the people out of Egypt.

Exodus 12:33-39; 13:17-22

God wanted His people to leave Egypt and go on a long trip to a new home. The people packed everything they had. They gathered all their animals. There were hundreds of thousands of people! That's more than you would want to count!

Moses told the people, "God will take care of us. God will lead us and show us the way."

During the day, God put a big, white cloud in the sky. The people followed the cloud. During the night, God put fire in the sky. The people followed the fire.

All of the people and animals walked behind God's cloud during the day and behind God's fire during the night. The people were glad they were going to a new home. They were glad God showed them He was with them. The people knew God was taking care of them on their long trip.

God makes a path through the Red Sea. Exodus 14:1-31

God makes a path through the Red Sea.

Exodus 14:1-31

Pharaoh wanted the Israelites to come back to Egypt. He didn't have enough slaves left to do all the work the Israelites had done before they left.

So Pharaoh and his army chased after the Israelites. When the people saw the army coming, they were afraid. They couldn't run away because they were at the edge of the Red Sea.

But God took care of His people. God told Moses to hold his hand out over the Red Sea. God sent a strong wind that blew and blew and made a path of dry land through the Red Sea. The people walked through the sea on dry ground!

The Egyptian army tried to follow them. When all the Israelites were safe on the other side, God told Moses to stretch his hand out over the sea again. The water went back into its place. Whoosh! The Egyptian army was covered up by the water.

All the Israelites trusted God because of the way He saved them from the Egyptians.

God gives manna to eat.

Exodus 16:1-36

God gives manna to eat.

Exodus 16:1-36

The people were hungry. They had been traveling in the desert for many days. They didn't have any more good food to eat. The people started to complain. They forgot that God would take care of them.

God told Moses that He was going to give His people food from heaven.

The next morning there were strange white flakes all around on the ground. "This is bread from the Lord," Moses told the people. The people called the bread manna. It tasted like crackers made with honey. All the people worked together to pick up the manna. Every day each person had enough to eat.

God gives the Ten Commandments.

Exodus 19:1—24:18

God gives the Ten Commandments.

Exodus 19:1—24:18

The Israelites walked in the desert for many days. They came to a mountain. God told them to camp by the mountain. All the people set up tents. They gathered fuel and made fires to cook food on. They found places for their animals to rest and eat.

God told Moses to come up to the top of the mountain. God wanted to talk with Moses. God told Moses many things while Moses was on the mountain. God gave Moses two stone tablets that God wrote His laws on. God told Moses many more laws for the people to follow. God's laws helped the people know what God wanted. God's laws told the people to be fair to each other.

Moses went down from the mountain and told the Israelites everything God had told him. The people promised to obey God.

The people bring gifts to make the Tabernacle.

Exodus 35:4—36:7

The people bring gifts to make the Tabernacle.

Exodus 35:4—36:7

God gave Moses plans to make a tent church called a Tabernacle. The Tabernacle was to be a special place to worship God. Moses told the people exactly how it should be made.

All the people who wanted to brought gifts of gold, precious stones and other things that were needed to make the Tabernacle. The people brought more and more beautiful things! It seemed that everyone wanted to give their very best things to help make the Tabernacle!

Soon there was enough to make the Tabernacle, but the people kept bringing more gifts. Finally, the men in charge of working on the Tabernacle went to see Moses. They said, "Tell the people to stop bringing gifts. We have too much!"

The people made the Tabernacle just as God told them.

Moses sends twelve spies to the Promised Land.

Numbers 13:1—14:35

Moses sends twelve spies to the Promised Land.

Numbers 13:1—14:35

Moses sent twelve men to explore the land God promised to give the Israelite people. The men looked at the cities and towns. They saw the good food that grew in the land. They saw the people who lived there.

The twelve men came back to Moses. They brought back some of the good food from the Promised Land. Ten of the men were scared. They said the people who lived in the land were too strong for them. They did not trust God to help them live in the land.

But two of the men, Joshua and Caleb, knew that God would keep His promise to give them the land. "Don't be afraid," they told the people. But the Israelites didn't believe Joshua and Caleb.

God said that because the people did not trust Him they would not be able to go to the Promised Land for a long time. The people would have to live in the desert for many years. But God promised that Joshua and Caleb would get to go to the Promised Land because they trusted God.

God provides water from a rock.
Numbers 20:1-13

God provides water from a rock.

Numbers 20:1-13

The people were thirsty. They came to Moses. "Why did you make us come out here to the desert?" they said. "Why did you make us leave Egypt? There is nothing good to eat here. There is no water."

Moses was angry with the people. They blamed him for all their problems. They forgot how God protected them and always cared for them. So Moses talked to God. God told Moses to speak to a rock in front of the people. God would make water come out of the rock.

Moses went to the rock. But Moses was so angry, he didn't do what God said. Instead of speaking to the rock, Moses hit the rock with his staff! God made water come out of the rock even though Moses didn't do what God said. God was sad that Moses didn't obey Him.

Rahab helps two spies.
Joshua 2:1-24

Rahab helps two spies.

Joshua 2:1-24

Joshua was the new leader of God's people. God told Joshua to lead the people into the Promised Land. God promised to be with Joshua. "Be strong and courageous," God said.

Joshua sent two spies to Jericho to look at the land. The king of Jericho heard about the spies and sent soldiers to find them. The spies were in the house of a woman named Rahab. She hid them on the roof of her house under some stalks of flax. When the soldiers came to her house, she told the soldiers that the men had already left the city.

The soldiers hurried out of the city to find the spies. Then Rahab helped the spies escape. Her house was on the wall of the city. The spies climbed down over the wall using a rope. Rahab asked the spies to keep her safe when they took over the land. The spies promised that no one in her house would be hurt if she left the rope hanging in the window.

The walls of Jericho fall down.

Joshua 6:1-27

The walls of Jericho fall down.

Joshua 6:1-27

Joshua and the Israelites were camped outside Jericho. The people of Jericho closed the gates to the city and didn't let anyone in or out. They were afraid. They didn't want the Israelites to take over their city.

God told Joshua a plan to take over the city. Joshua and the Israelites did just what God said. Very quietly, they stood in a line. They didn't say a word. They marched all the way around Jericho. They did this every day for almost a whole week.

On the last day, they marched around the city one, two, three, four, five, six, seven times. Then they stopped. The priests blew the trumpets and all the people shouted. Then the walls fell down flat! The Israelites marched straight into the city.

Deborah helps Barak.

Judges 4:1—5:31

Deborah helps Barak.

Judges 4:1—5:31

Deborah talked to Barak. She said, "God wants you to lead an army. God is going to win the battle." But Barak didn't want to go alone. He wanted Deborah to help him lead the army. He said, "If you don't go with me, I won't go."

So Deborah said that she would go with Barak. They led an army of Israelites to the side of a mountain. The Israelites camped on the mountain. The Caananite army had many chariots and fast horses. The Caananites started to attack the Israelites in a dried-out river below the mountain.

At just the right time, God sent a big storm. It rained so much and so fast that the Caananites' chariots got stuck in the mud. Their fast horses couldn't run away.

Deborah told Barak, "Go! God has made you the winner!" The Caananite army couldn't fight. They couldn't get away. Deborah and Barak won the battle because God helped them.

An angel talks to Gideon.

Judges 6:1-24

An angel talks to Gideon.

Judges 6:1-24

The Midianites were the Israelites' enemies. They stole everything from the Israelites! The Israelites were so afraid they hid in caves in the mountains. The Israelites asked God to help them.

One day an Israelite named Gideon was hiding from the Midianites. Gideon was hiding because he didn't want the Midianites to come and steal the wheat he was threshing.

Suddenly an angel appeared and said, "The Lord is with you, mighty warrior." What a funny way to talk to someone who was hiding!

God told Gideon to save Israel from the Midianites. Gideon didn't think that he could save Israel, but God said that He would go with Gideon and help him. Gideon still wasn't sure, so he asked the angel to prove he was speaking from God. The angel did! After that, Gideon did what the angel told him to do.

God helps Gideon defeat the Midianites.

Judges 7:1-21

God helps Gideon defeat the Midianites.

Judges 7:1-21

Many people came to help Gideon fight the Midianites. But many of the men were afraid. "Let everyone who is afraid go home," God told Gideon. Most of the men left.

But God thought Gideon's army was still too big. God told Gideon to take the men to the river to get a drink. Most of the men got down on their knees to drink. God told Gideon to send those men home.

Now only three hundred men were left. That was not very many! The army from Midian had more men than Gideon could count. There was no way that only three hundred men could win a battle against such a big army!

God told Gideon what to do. Gideon gave each man in his army a trumpet and a jar with a torch inside. The men surrounded the Midianite camp.

At just the right time they blew their trumpets, broke their jars and shouted, "The sword of the Lord and Gideon!" When the big Midianite army heard the noise and saw the lights, they ran away! God saved His people with a small army and a leader who obeyed God.

Ruth shows love.
Ruth 1:1-22

Ruth shows love.

Ruth 1:1-22

Naomi and her family lived in Israel. But there wasn't much food in Israel anymore. So Naomi and her family went to live in Moab. There was plenty of food in Moab.

Naomi's two sons grew up and got married. One of them married Ruth. After a while, Naomi's sons and husband died. Naomi was sad. She heard that there was food in Israel again, so she decided to go home.

Ruth wanted to go with Naomi. "Stay here in Moab," Naomi said. "I don't have any money. You would be poor if you stayed with me."

"Please don't tell me to leave you," Ruth said. "I will go wherever you go. Your people will be my people and your God my God." Ruth stayed with Naomi because she loved Naomi and she loved God. Ruth didn't mind that they were very poor and didn't have any way to make money.

Ruth helps Naomi.
Ruth 2:1—4:22

Ruth helps Naomi.

Ruth 2:1—4:22

Ruth and Naomi didn't have any money. They couldn't buy any food. They needed some grain to make bread to eat.

Ruth went to a field where some workers were harvesting grain. She picked up the grain that the workers left behind. It was hard work. It took a long time to find enough food this way.

A man named Boaz owned the field where Ruth went to gather grain. Boaz was very kind to Ruth. He invited her to eat lunch with his workers. He told his workers to help Ruth. The workers made sure to leave lots of extra grain for Ruth to find.

Ruth brought the grain to Naomi to be made into bread. Naomi was glad Ruth helped her have food to eat. Ruth and Naomi were glad to have a friend like Boaz. After a while, Ruth and Boaz got married. God took care of Ruth and Naomi.

Samson is strong.

Judges 13:1-25; 16:1-22

Samson is strong.

Judges 13:1-25; 16:1-22

An angel told a man and woman that they were going to have a special baby. The angel told them that this baby should serve God all his life. The angel gave them special rules for this baby to follow. One of the rules was that he should never cut his hair.

The baby's name was Samson. After Samson was born, God helped him grow up strong. Samson fought the Philistines, who were hurting the Israelites. Samson became so strong that he could defeat entire armies by himself! Samson could break thick ropes as if they were strings and kill lions with his bare hands.

One day Samson let a woman called Delilah trick him. He told her how to make his strength go away. While Samson slept, Delilah called to the Philistines. She told them to cut off Samson's hair. When Samson's hair was cut, Samson woke up. Samson thought that he would still be strong, but the strength that God gave him was gone because he didn't obey God. The Philistines took him as their prisoner.

God answers Hannah's prayer.

1 Samuel 1:1—2:11

God answers Hannah's prayer.

1 Samuel 1:1—2:11

Hannah's husband had another wife named Peninnah. Peninnah had sons and daughters, but Hannah didn't have any children. Peninnah made fun of Hannah because she didn't have children. Hannah felt sad.

When Hannah's family went to worship God at the Tabernacle, Hannah cried and cried. She prayed, "Please God, give me a son."

Eli, the priest, saw Hannah praying and thought she was drunk. He told Hannah to stop getting drunk. Hannah said, "I am not drunk. I am very sad and am asking God to help me." Eli told her to go in peace. Eli asked God to give her what she asked for.

God answered Hannah's prayer. Hannah named her baby boy Samuel. When he was old enough, Hannah took Samuel to the Tabernacle so that he could serve God.

God speaks to Samuel.

1 Samuel 3:1-21

God speaks to Samuel.

1 Samuel 3:1-21

Eli, the priest, was getting old. Samuel helped Eli take care of the Tabernacle. Samuel slept on a mat on the floor of the Tabernacle. One night Samuel heard a voice calling his name. Samuel jumped up and ran to where Eli was sleeping. "Here I am. You called me."

Eli said, "I didn't call you. Go back to sleep." Samuel went back to his mat on the floor. Soon, Samuel heard the voice again. Samuel quickly ran to Eli again, but Eli hadn't called him. Samuel went back to his mat again. But he heard the voice again! Samuel thought it had to be Eli calling! There was no one else who would call him in the middle of the night. Samuel ran to Eli. Eli realized that God was calling Samuel. God must have something important to tell Samuel.

Eli told Samuel to go back and lie down. Eli said, "If He calls you, say 'Speak, Lord, for your servant is listening.'" Samuel did what Eli said. God told Samuel what He was going to do. Samuel listened to God.

Samuel chooses a king.

1 Samuel 8:1—10:24

Samuel chooses a king.

1 Samuel 8:1—10:24

Samuel grew up to be the leader of Israel. He was called a judge. Now Samuel was getting old. Some people talked to Samuel. They said, "Give us a king like all the other countries around us. We want to be like them."

Samuel was upset because he knew God was the real King of Israel! So he prayed to God. God said, "Samuel, warn them. Tell them that a king will make them his servants and will take their land and animals."

Samuel told the people all the things God had said. The people didn't care! They said, "We want a king anyway!"

About that time, a young man named Saul was out looking for his father's lost donkeys. As Saul walked into town, Samuel saw Saul. God said, "Samuel, here's the man I want to be king."

Samuel said to Saul, "I'd like you to come and eat with me. And don't worry, your donkeys have been found." The next morning, Samuel took a small bottle of olive oil and poured it on Saul's head saying, "The Lord has chosen you to be the leader of His people." And from that time, God helped Saul become ready to be king.

David plays his harp for King Saul.

1 Samuel 16:14-23

David plays his harp for King Saul.

1 Samuel 16:14-23

King Saul sat on his throne. He didn't want to talk to anyone. He didn't want to do anything. King Saul felt sad. The king's servants were worried. They wanted to make the king feel better. What could the servants do? What might make the king feel better?

"Maybe some music would help," one of the servants said.

Another servant said, "There is a shepherd boy named David who is a good musician. He is a brave and handsome young man. He loves God. David could play his harp for the king."

King Saul sent a messenger to David's father. "Send David here so he can work for me." David's father sent David to King Saul. Whenever King Saul felt sad, David played the harp for him. Then King Saul would feel better.

David fights Goliath.
1 Samuel 17:1-58

David fights Goliath.

1 Samuel 17:1-58

David's brothers were in Saul's army. One day, David's father sent him to visit his brothers. David saw the army getting ready to fight the Philistines. Suddenly, a giant Philistine came out. Saul's army was afraid. They ran back to their tents.

Goliath, the Philistine giant, was more than nine feet tall. Goliath yelled, "Choose a man to fight me. If he is able to kill me, we will become your slaves. But if I win the fight, you will become our slaves." No one in the Israelite camp wanted to fight Goliath. They didn't think anyone could beat someone so big!

David knew that God was stronger than Goliath. David said, "I'll go and fight him." King Saul heard what David said. "You're too young and small to fight Goliath," King Saul said.

"But God helped me fight lions and bears when I took care of my father's sheep, and God will help me now," David answered.

Goliath laughed when he saw David. He even made fun of God! David used just his slingshot and a stone to fight Goliath. God helped David save his people from the Philistine army.

David and Jonathan are friends.

1 Samuel 18:1-4; 20:1-42

David and Jonathan are friends.

1 Samuel 18:1-4; 20:1-42

"Hooray for David!" All the women danced and sang, "David is a great warrior!" Everyone loved David. Even King Saul's son, Prince Jonathan, liked David. Jonathan knew that David loved God, and that David was a brave warrior. Jonathan wanted David to be his good friend. Jonathan gave David some gifts. David and Jonathan even promised to remain good friends whatever happened in the future.

King Saul made David an officer in the army. Whenever the king sent David on a mission, David did a great job. God always helped David. But King Saul was not happy. King Saul was jealous of David. Saul was afraid that his people would want David to be king instead!

David found out that the king wanted to hurt him, so David ran away and hid. Later he talked to Jonathan. Jonathan and David were very sad. Jonathan helped David get away from King Saul. David promised to always be kind to Jonathan and his children.

David doesn't hurt Saul.

1 Samuel 24:1-22

King Saul and his men chased David. David and his men quietly hid in the back of a deep dark cave. They didn't say a word. Saul and his men were right outside the cave! They didn't know where David was.

King Saul went inside the cave by himself. He thought the cave was empty.

Inside the cave, David's men said, "Now you can stop King Saul from chasing you. You can kill him and become king."

David crept up next to King Saul. David cut off the corner of King Saul's robe. David didn't hurt the king. King Saul didn't even know that David was there.

After King Saul left the cave, David came out and called to him. David showed the king the corner of the robe that David had cut off. David said, "Why are you chasing me? I have not done anything wrong." King Saul felt sorry for being mean to David. King Saul stopped chasing David for a while.

Abigail is wise.

1 Samuel 25:2-42

Abigail is wise.

1 Samuel 25:2-42

David and his men lived in the desert. A man named Nabal lived there, too. Nabal had many sheep and goats. Every day the sheep and the goats ate grass and drank water near the place where David and his men were. David's men could have stolen some of them. But instead, David and his men made sure that everything Nabal had stayed safe.

One day David sent some of his men to see Nabal. Nabal should have given them some of his food to tell David thank you for being kind to him. Nabal didn't give them anything. Nabal even said very bad things about David!

David was angry. David and his men got ready to go hurt Nabal. Nabal's wife, Abigail, heard what happened. Abigail gathered lots of food. She quickly put the food on some donkeys. Abigail and her servants went to meet David. "I'm sorry. I didn't see the men you sent," Abigail said. "Don't pay any attention to what Nabal said. He was wrong."

David was glad Abigail kept him from doing something mean when he felt angry. David thanked God for Abigail.

King Solomon is wise.

1 Kings 3:1-15

King Solomon is wise.

1 Kings 3:1-15

Solomon was the new king. Solomon knew that it would not be easy to be a good and fair king. He knew that he needed God to help him. King Solomon went to a special place to worship God.

That night, while Solomon was sleeping, he had a dream. In his dream, God told Solomon to ask for whatever he wanted. Solomon didn't ask for money. He didn't ask for a long life. He didn't even ask to become famous. Solomon asked God to make him wise so he could be a good king.

God was happy that Solomon asked for wisdom. God knew that Solomon was more concerned about doing what was right than about getting rich. God made a promise to Solomon. "Since you asked for wisdom and not for long life or money," God said, "I will make you more wise than anyone else. I will also give you riches and honor." The Bible says Solomon was the wisest person who ever lived.

Solomon builds the Temple.

1 Kings 5:1—6:38; 7:13-51; 2 Chronicles 2:1—4:22

Solomon builds the Temple.

1 Kings 5:1—6:38; 7:13-51; 2 Chronicles 2:1—4:22

King Solomon wanted to build a Temple for God. The Temple would be a place for people to come to pray and learn about God. King Solomon hired many people to work on the Temple. There were people who carried wood, people who cut giant stones, people who carved beautiful designs in the wood, and even people who put pure gold over everything!

King Solomon also had skilled craftsmen make many beautiful gold and bronze things to put in the Temple. There were tables and lampstands, dishes and pillars, stands and basins. It was a wonderful Temple! Inside, everything glittered with gold. From the outside, you could see giant pillars and beautiful decorations.

After everything was finished, King Solomon called all the people of Israel to come to the Temple. They all thanked God and had a big celebration.

God sends ravens with food for Elijah.

1 Kings 17:1-6

God sends ravens with food for Elijah.

1 Kings 17:1-6

Ahab was the new king of Israel. Ahab didn't worship God. Ahab built places to worship idols instead of God. Many of the people in Israel stopped worshiping God because of the evil things that Ahab did. God was angry with Ahab.

Elijah didn't worship idols. Elijah obeyed God. Elijah went to see King Ahab. "There won't be any rain for a long time," Elijah said. "There won't be any rain to make the food in the fields grow. There won't be any rain to make the grass green. There won't be any rain to give the people water to drink." Ahab was very angry.

So God told Elijah to hide from the king. Elijah left the city. He walked and walked. Elijah came to a brook. Elijah drank some water from the brook. God told Elijah to stay by the brook. God told Elijah that birds called ravens were going to bring food to him. Every morning and every evening the ravens came with bread and meat for Elijah to eat.

**God answers
Elijah's prayer.**

1 Kings 18:16-39

God answers Elijah's prayer.

1 Kings 18:16-39

Many Israelites stopped worshiping God. They worshiped idols instead. Elijah said, "How long will you do this? Worship the one true God!" But the people didn't listen.

Elijah challenged the prophets of Baal (a false god) to have a contest. Elijah said, "The God who sends fire from heaven is the real God." The people thought the contest was a good idea. They wanted to see whether God or Baal could send fire from heaven.

The prophets of Baal began asking Baal to send fire. They danced and prayed. Baal could not send fire. Baal was not God. Baal was an idol the people made. He couldn't do anything.

Then it was Elijah's turn. First Elijah repaired an old altar where people used to worship the one true God. Elijah dug a trench around the altar. Elijah had some men pour lots of water on the altar. Elijah prayed. God sent fire from heaven. The fire burned up everything that was on the altar. The fire even burned up all the water the men had poured on the altar. Now the people knew who the real God was. The people worshiped God.

Elijah goes to heaven.

2 Kings 2:1-14

Elijah goes to heaven.

2 Kings 2:1-14

Elijah was an important prophet who told people messages from God. But it was time for Elijah to leave and go to heaven. Elijah and Elisha walked together. They crossed a river. Elijah said, "If God lets you see me when I go up to heaven, then you will take over my job."

Suddenly a chariot and some horses that looked like fire swooped down out of the sky! Then Elijah went to heaven in a whirlwind. All that was left was Elijah's cloak that had fallen to the ground. Elisha picked up the cloak.

Elisha had seen the chariot and the horses. It was very exciting! Elisha was sad that Elijah was not going to be with him anymore, but now Elisha had an important job to do. Elisha knew God was with him and would help him.

Elisha helps a widow.
2 Kings 4:1-7

Elisha helps a widow.

2 Kings 4:1-7

A woman's husband died. The woman had no money to pay her bills. The bill collector said, "Give me your two sons so I can sell them as slaves and get my money back."

The woman asked Elisha for help. Elisha asked, "What do you have in your house?" The woman said, "I don't have anything except a little oil."

"Go ask your neighbors to give you empty jars," Elisha said. "Get as many jars as you can. Then go inside your house and shut the door. Pour oil into all the jars." The woman and her sons did exactly what Elisha said.

The woman took her little jar of oil and began to pour oil into the jars. She filled up one jar, then another and another. She kept pouring oil until all the jars were full! When all the jars were full, the oil stopped flowing out of her jar. The woman knew that only God could fill all those jars with oil from her little jar!

Elisha told the woman to sell the jars of oil and use the money to pay what she owed. She did what Elisha told her to, and she even had some money left over!

**Naaman
is healed.**

2 Kings 5:1-19

Naaman is healed.

2 Kings 5:1-19

Naaman was an important commander in the army. But his skin had a terrible disease. He needed to get well. Naaman's servant girl told him, "Elisha, God's prophet, could help you." Naaman gathered gold and silver and nice clothes. Naaman took the gifts to Elisha. Naaman wanted Elisha to do something special to make him well. But Elisha didn't even talk to Naaman. Elisha sent his servant to talk to Naaman. Elisha's servant told Naaman to take a bath in the Jordan River seven times.

Naaman was angry. The Jordan River was muddy! Naaman didn't think doing what Elisha said would help him get well. Naaman started to go home. But Naaman's servants begged him to do what Elisha's servant said. Naaman didn't want to, but he did it anyway. Naaman went under the water one, two, three, four, five, six, seven times.

Now Naaman's skin was healthy! Naaman was happy. He went back to Elisha's house. Naaman said, "Please take these presents." Elisha said, "No, God made you well. I just serve God." Naaman promised to worship God, too.

Elisha leads a blind army.

2 Kings 6:8-23

Elisha leads a blind army.

2 Kings 6:8-23

A king was angry with Elisha because Elisha helped the king's enemies. The king sent an army to capture Elisha. The army came at night. They surrounded the town where Elisha was sleeping. The army waited. In the morning, Elisha's servant saw the army. He was afraid. Elisha's servant said, "Oh, no! What will we do?"

"Don't be afraid," Elisha said. Elisha prayed for his servant. Then Elisha's servant saw horses and chariots that looked like fire all around the enemy army. Elisha's servant knew that God was taking care of them. Then Elisha prayed again. This time he prayed that God would make the enemy army blind.

Elisha led the blind army to the city where the king of Israel was. Then Elisha prayed that God would let the army see again. The men in the army looked and saw that they were trapped! The soldiers of Israel were all around them. Elisha said to the king of Israel, "Give these people food and water and then let them go back home." Elisha was kind to the army that came to capture him. The army stopped being mean to Elisha's people for a while.

Joash repairs the Temple.

2 Kings 12:1-15; 2 Chronicles 24:1-14

Joash repairs the Temple.

2 Kings 12:1-15; 2 Chronicles 24:1-14

No one cleaned up the Temple anymore. The Temple was dirty. Many things inside the Temple were broken. Some important things were missing. The walls and roof needed to be repaired.

King Joash wanted to fix the Temple. He told the priests to use the money that people brought to fix the Temple.

The priests put a large box by the altar so everyone could put money in it to help fix the Temple. Whenever the box got full, the priests would empty the box. They gave the money to the men who were fixing the Temple. The men worked hard and did their best. All the people wanted the Temple to look nice again. The people wanted to use the Temple to worship God and to learn more about Him.

Hezekiah praises God.

2 Chronicles 30:1-27

Hezekiah praises God.

2 Chronicles 30:1-27

King Hezekiah knew it had been a long, long time since God's people had come to the Temple to worship God. One day King Hezekiah sent an important letter to all God's people. The king's helpers took the letter to all the cities where God's people lived. "Come to the beautiful Temple," the letter said.

The people were so excited! Everyone wanted to go to the Temple. As the people came, King Hezekiah said, "Come, let us worship the Lord God together." The people sang happy songs about God. The leaders read God's words from the big scrolls. And the people prayed to God.

God's people stayed at the Temple for seven days. When it was time to go home, they said to King Hezekiah, "We do not want to go home yet." So they stayed seven more days. Everyone had a happy time singing and praying to God.

Jonah disobeys God.

Jonah 1:1—2:10

Jonah disobeys God.

Jonah 1:1—2:10

God was not happy with the way the people in Nineveh acted. God told Jonah to warn the people in Nineveh that God would punish them for all the bad things they kept doing. But Jonah didn't like the people in Nineveh and didn't want them to get a warning. So Jonah decided to disobey God. Jonah got on a boat that was going the other way.

God wanted Jonah to obey Him. God sent a storm that made the boat start to sink. The people on the boat were afraid. Jonah said, "God sent this storm because I ran away from Him. If you want this storm to stop, you must throw me overboard." The people on the boat threw Jonah into the water. Suddenly, the sea was still.

Jonah went down, down, down. Jonah wanted to breathe, but he couldn't. Jonah saw a giant fish swimming toward him! Jonah tried to swim away, but the giant fish opened its giant mouth and swallowed Jonah. Gulp!

Jonah was in the belly of the big fish. Now Jonah could breathe. It must have been very smelly! Jonah was sorry he had disobeyed God. He prayed and promised to obey God. Finally, God made the fish swim to the shore and spit Jonah up on the beach.

Jonah preaches in Nineveh.

Jonah 3:1-10

Jonah preaches in Nineveh.

Jonah 3:1-10

God told Jonah, "Go to Nineveh and tell the people there about me." Jonah didn't obey God the first time God told him to go. But, after spending three days inside a giant fish, Jonah did what God said.

Jonah went to the big city of Nineveh. Jonah started to walk through the city. Jonah walked one day. Jonah walked two days. Jonah walked three days. As he walked, Jonah told the people about God.

The people of Nineveh listened to Jonah. They knew that they had done wrong things. They knew that God was not happy. The people of Nineveh were very sorry. They stopped eating. They didn't wear their fancy clothes. They stopped doing wrong things. They asked God to forgive them. God was happy that the people of Nineveh listened to Him. God forgave them for doing wrong things.

Josiah hears God's Word.

2 Kings 22:1—23:3; 2 Chronicles 34:14-32

Josiah hears God's Word.

2 Kings 22:1—23:3; 2 Chronicles 34:14-32

Josiah was only eight years old when he became king. No one in his country read God's Word anymore. Even the priests who were in charge of the Temple didn't know where God's Word was!

One day a priest in the Temple found a scroll with God's Word written on it. He ran to the king's helper. "Here is a scroll with God's Word written on it!" the priest said. "King Josiah will want to see this!" The helper took the scroll to the king.

The king's helper read God's Word to Josiah. King Josiah listened to God's Word. King Josiah loved God and wanted to obey God's Word, but when he heard what was written in God's Word, he cried. It made him sad to learn that his people were not obeying God.

King Josiah called all the leaders together. He told them what God's Word said. Josiah and all the leaders promised to obey God's Word.

The king destroys the scroll of God's Words.

Jeremiah 36:1-32

The King destroys the scroll of God's Words.

Jeremiah 36:1-32

God told Jeremiah some things to write down. Jeremiah called his friend Baruch to write down the words God told Jeremiah. Baruch carefully wrote down everything Jeremiah told him.

Then Jeremiah told Baruch to take the scroll he had written on and read it in the Temple so all the people could hear God's words. Some men who worked for the king heard what Baruch read. They asked Baruch to give them the scroll. Then they told Baruch and Jeremiah to go and hide, because they knew the king would be angry when he heard God's words.

The men who worked for the king took the scroll and read it to the king. The king didn't want to hear what God said. The king cut up the scroll and threw it in the fire! The king tried to put Baruch and Jeremiah in jail, but God protected them. Then God told Jeremiah to tell Baruch to write the words down again. Those words are still in our Bible today!

Daniel and his friends choose to obey God.

Daniel 1:1-21

Daniel and his friends choose to obey God.

Daniel 1:1-21

Daniel and his friends were taken to a faraway palace. The king wanted them to learn to work for him. The king gave them some special food. Daniel and his friends knew that God did not want them to eat the kind of food that the king gave them.

Daniel and his friends wanted to obey God. Daniel asked the king's helper to give his friends and him only vegetables and water. The king's helper was afraid that Daniel and his friends would not be as healthy as some of the other boys who were learning to work for the king. The king's helper knew that the king would be angry if Daniel and his friends were not healthy.

Daniel said, "Please test us for ten days. Give us only vegetables and water and then see who is healthiest—my friends and I or the others." The king's helper agreed to test them.

After ten days, Daniel and his friends looked healthier than any of the other young men. God helped Daniel and his friends. The king liked Daniel and his friends. He gave them important jobs.

God protects Daniel's friends in a furnace.

Daniel 3:1-30

God protects Daniel's friends in a furnace.

Daniel 3:1-30

King Nebuchadnezzar built a tall, tall statue. King Nebuchadnezzar wanted everyone to bow down and worship his statue. The king said, "Anyone who does not bow down will be thrown into a blazing furnace!"

Some men who worked for the king saw that Shadrach, Meshach and Abednego did not bow down to the king's statue. They did not bow down because they knew they should only worship God, not a statue.

The king was very angry with the three men. The king ordered his guards to tie up Shadrach, Meshach and Abednego and throw them into the hottest furnace. But when they were in the furnace, the king saw something very strange. Shadrach, Meshach and Abednego were not being burned up! They were not even tied up anymore. They were walking around inside the furnace with another person—an angel!

The king called to Shadrach, Meshach and Abednego, "Servants of the Most High God, come out!" The king said, "Praise God who sent an angel to save His servants. Shadrach, Meshach and Abednego would rather give up their lives than worship any god other than the one true God."

God protects Daniel in a den of lions. Daniel 6:1-28

God protects Daniel in a den of lions.

Daniel 6:1-28

Daniel loved God and prayed to Him every day. In fact, he prayed three times every day. Daniel knew that praying to God was a right thing to do.

There were some mean men who did not like Daniel. They went to the king and said, "King, we think you should make a rule that everyone must pray only to you. If people pray to anyone else but you, they will be thrown into a cave filled with lions!" The king thought this was a good idea.

The next day Daniel prayed to God. The mean men watched as Daniel prayed to God. Then they ran to tell the king what they saw.

The king was sad. Daniel was his friend. The king knew he had been tricked into hurting Daniel. But the king had to obey the rule, too. Daniel was put into a big cave where hungry lions lived.

All night the king worried about Daniel. The next morning, the king ran to the lions' cave. He called, "Daniel! Daniel!" Daniel called out, "King, I am safe. The Lord God took care of me!"

The king was so glad that Daniel was not hurt. Then the king told everyone what God had done.

Esther is chosen queen.

Esther 2:1-18

Esther is chosen queen.

Esther 2:1-18

The queen didn't do what King Xerxes wanted. The king was very angry. "What should I do?" the king asked his friends.

The king's friends said, "Send her away and find a new queen." So the king started looking for a new queen. Many beautiful girls in the kingdom were brought to the palace.

One girl who was brought to the palace was named Esther. Esther was very beautiful. Esther met the king. The king liked Esther. The king said, "I want Esther to be the new queen." The king put a crown on Esther's head. The king invited many people to a banquet for Queen Esther. The king was so happy that he told everyone to take a holiday. The king didn't know that God had a special job for Esther to do.

Queen Esther saves her people.

Esther 4:1—7:10

Queen Esther saves her people.

Esther 4:1—7:10

Haman had an evil plan. He tricked King Xerxes into making a law to kill all the Jewish people. The king and Haman didn't know that Queen Esther was Jewish. Queen Esther had to ask the king to save her people.

It was against the law for anyone to go to the king unless he wanted to see that person. Queen Esther was afraid the king would be angry with her, so she asked all her people to pray and stop eating for three days. After three days, Esther went to see the king. The king was happy to see her!

Queen Esther invited the king to a banquet. She also invited Haman. After two banquets, Esther asked the king to save her people. The king was angry. He asked, "Who wanted to hurt my queen?"

"It's Haman," Esther answered. The king let Esther write a new law to protect Jewish people. The king gave everything Haman owned to Esther and had Haman put to death. The Jews were saved!

Nehemiah rebuilds the walls.

Nehemiah 2:11—4:23

Nehemiah rebuilds the walls.

Nehemiah 2:11—4:23

Nehemiah was the king's special helper. One day, Nehemiah's brother came from far away to visit him. "The city where we used to live had strong walls. Now they are broken. The city is not safe."

Nehemiah was sad. So Nehemiah prayed to God.

When the king saw Nehemiah he asked him, "Why are you so sad?" Nehemiah said, "I am sad because the wall around my city is broken down."

The king said, "You may go and help the people build the wall. Come back when it is finished." Nehemiah was very happy.

When Nehemiah came to the city, he said to all the people, "We can build the wall. We can make it strong again."

Everyone worked together. After many days, the wall was finished. Everyone was glad to see the wall. And Nehemiah was glad God had heard his prayer.

An angel visits Mary.

Luke 1:26-38

An angel visits Mary.

Luke 1:26-38

God wanted to tell a girl named Mary some good news. When you tell someone good news, you might call on the telephone or write a letter. But God sent an angel to talk to Mary!

One day Mary was alone. She looked up. Standing right there beside her was an angel! Mary had never seen a real angel before. Mary was surprised to see the angel. She was afraid.

The angel said, "Don't be afraid, Mary. God loves you. He has chosen you to be the mother of a very special baby. You will name the baby Jesus. This special baby will be God's own Son!"

Mary was glad to hear this promise. She praised God.

Jesus is born.
Luke 2:1-7

Jesus is born.

Luke 2:1-7

Mary was going to have a baby. An angel had come to tell Mary about this baby. Her baby would be special. He would be God's Son.

When it was time to have her baby, Mary and Joseph had to take a trip. They walked and walked for three days. Finally Mary and Joseph came to Bethlehem. There were so many people that there weren't any rooms left in the inn. There wasn't anywhere else for them to stay.

Finally, Mary and Joseph found a place to stay. It wasn't a nice place. It probably wasn't even a clean place. It was a place for animals to stay! Mary's little baby was born there. Mary wrapped the little baby in some clean cloths and then she laid Him in a manger filled with clean straw. Mary and Joseph named this baby Jesus.

Angels tell the good news of Jesus' birth to shepherds.

Luke 2:8-20

Angels tell the good news of Jesus' birth to shepherds.

Luke 2:8-20

On the night Jesus was born, some shepherds were out in the fields near Bethlehem, taking care of their sheep. It was dark and quiet. Suddenly the shepherds saw an angel! The shepherds were terrified! The angel said, "Don't be afraid. I have good news for you and for everyone else. The Savior has been born in Bethlehem. You will find the baby wrapped in cloths and lying in a manger."

As soon as the angel finished talking, the sky was full of angels. They were all praising God and saying, "Glory to God in the highest, and peace on earth."

Then, suddenly, the angels were gone. The shepherds looked at each other. They said, "Let's go to Bethlehem and see this baby!" They ran to Bethlehem and found baby Jesus lying in a manger. The shepherds were so happy that they told everyone they saw about Jesus. They praised God for sending Jesus!

Wise men come to worship.
Matthew 2:1-12

Wise men come to worship.

Matthew 2:1-12

Wise men in a country far from Bethlehem watched the sky and tried to learn things from the stars. God put a new star in the sky so the wise men would know that Jesus was born.

The wise men traveled to Jerusalem. "Where is this new king of the Jews? We saw his star in the sky and have come to worship him," the wise men said. The priests and teachers looked in the scrolls that told about Jesus coming. The scrolls said this new king of the Jews was to be born in Bethlehem.

The wise men went to Bethlehem. The star they had seen in the sky went ahead of them and stopped over the house where Jesus was. The wise men were very happy. They went into the house, bowed down and worshiped Jesus. Then the wise men gave gifts to Jesus.

Jesus escapes to Egypt.
Matthew 2:13-23

Jesus escapes to Egypt.

Matthew 2:13-23

Joseph and Mary and little Jesus were asleep in their house. Joseph had a dream. In the dream, an angel told Joseph to get up quickly and take Mary and little Jesus to Egypt. The angel said that Jesus was in danger because King Herod wanted to kill Him! Joseph got up. He and Mary packed what they needed. They quickly left Bethlehem with Jesus. They traveled all the way to Egypt.

After they left, King Herod sent his soldiers to Bethlehem, the town where Jesus was born. King Herod told his soldiers to kill all the little boys in Bethlehem! It was a horrible thing for the king to do. The king was a very mean man. But Jesus was safe. God had protected Jesus.

Joseph and Mary and baby Jesus stayed in Egypt until the king died. Then an angel came and told Joseph that it was safe for them to go back home. They went to live in Nazareth.

Mary and Joseph look for Jesus.

Luke 2:41-52

Mary and Joseph look for Jesus.

Luke 2:41-52

Crowds of people were on their way home. They had been to Jerusalem for a special celebration. Mary and Joseph were there. They were walking and talking with their friends. They thought Jesus was there in the crowd, too. They thought Jesus was walking and talking with His friends.

Mary and Joseph and their friends walked all day. When it began to get dark, Mary and Joseph started looking for Jesus. *Jesus should be here somewhere* Mary must have thought. Mary and Joseph did not find Jesus. Mary and Joseph were worried. *What happened to Jesus? Did He get hurt? Is He lost?*

They hurried back to Jerusalem. Mary and Joseph looked and looked. Finally they found Jesus. He was sitting in the Temple! Jesus was listening to the teachers. Jesus was asking them questions. The teachers were amazed at Jesus. The teachers were learning from Jesus even though He was just a boy. Mary asked Jesus, "Why are you here? We have been looking for you."

Jesus said, "Why were you looking for me? Didn't you know I had to be in my Father's house?" Jesus went home with Mary and Joseph. Jesus obeyed them.

John the Baptist preaches about the coming Savior.
Matthew 3:1-12; Mark 1:1-8; Luke 3:1-20

John the Baptist preaches about the coming Savior.

Matthew 3:1-12; Mark 1:1-8; Luke 3:1-20

Many people went to the desert. It was hot. People walked a long way. Why did all those people go to the desert? They went to see a preacher: John the Baptist. John the Baptist wore clothes made out of camel's hair. His clothes must have been very itchy!

John the Baptist ate locusts (like big grasshoppers) and wild honey. He didn't have good food like you and I have. John the Baptist didn't care about nice clothes or good-tasting food. John the Baptist cared about telling the people that the Savior of the world was coming.

John told the people to stop doing wrong things and start doing good things. John said, "Share your food with people who don't have any. Don't cheat people or steal from them any more. Be happy with what you have." John said that people needed to be ready because Jesus was coming soon.

John baptizes Jesus.

Matthew 3:13-17; Mark 1:9-11;
Luke 3:21,22; John 1:29-34

John baptizes Jesus.

Matthew 3:13-17; Mark 1:9-11; Luke 3:21,22; John 1:29-34

One day Jesus went to see John the Baptist. John was preaching and baptizing people in the Jordan River. John told people to turn away from doing bad things because the Savior of the world was coming.

Jesus asked John to baptize Him. John knew that Jesus was the Savior of the world. John said, "I am not even good enough to tie your shoes. Why do you ask me to baptize you? You ought to baptize me!" Jesus said that it was right for John to baptize Him.

So John and Jesus waded out into the river. After John baptized Jesus, a dove flew down and landed on Jesus to show that God was with Him. A voice from heaven said, "This is my Son. I am pleased with Him."

When Jesus is tempted, He obeys God's Word.

Matthew 4:1-11; Mark 1:12,13; Luke 4:1-13

When Jesus is tempted, He obeys God's Word.

Matthew 4:1-11; Mark 1:12,13; Luke 4:1-13

One day, Jesus went to a quiet, lonely place in the desert. Jesus was getting ready to do important work for God. Jesus stayed in the desert for 40 days. He did not eat anything the whole time!

At the end of 40 days, God's enemy, Satan, came to see Jesus. Satan wanted Jesus to do something that was wrong.

Satan knew Jesus was very hungry. Satan showed Jesus a stone. "If you want to, you can turn this stone into bread," Satan said. But Jesus told Satan that real life comes from God's Word and is even more important than eating. Jesus knew He shouldn't do what Satan wanted Him to do.

Satan did not give up. Satan took Jesus to the top of a very tall building. "You can prove to everyone you are God's Son," Satan said. "If You jump off this building, angels will come and save You." But Jesus said no. He was not going to do something foolish just to prove God's love for Him.

Satan still did not give up. Satan took Jesus to the top of a very high mountain. He showed Jesus the whole world. "If You worship me instead of God, I will give You this whole world," Satan said to Jesus.

Jesus said, "No! The Bible says people should only worship God." Satan tempted Jesus, but Jesus did what was right. Jesus obeyed God's Word.

Jesus says, "Follow me."

Matthew 4:18-22; Mark 1:16-20; Luke 5:1-11; John 1:40-42

Jesus says, "Follow me."

Matthew 4:18-22; Mark 1:16-20; Luke 5:1-11; John 1:40-42

Peter and Andrew liked to fish. They went fishing every day. Fishing was how they earned money.

One day Jesus came to the Sea of Galilee where they were fishing. Many people wanted to hear Jesus teach. The people kept crowding around Him, trying to get closer. Jesus got into Peter and Andrew's boat. Then Jesus sat down and taught all the people who were crowded on the beach.

When Jesus finished talking to the people, Jesus told Peter to take the boat out into deeper water. Then Jesus told Peter to let down his nets to catch some fish.

When Peter and Andrew let down the nets, they caught so many fish that the nets began to break! Peter and Andrew called to their partners in another boat to come and help them. There were so many fish that when they pulled the nets with the fish into the boats, the boats began to sink. Quickly, the men rowed to shore.

Jesus said, "From now on you will catch people." Jesus meant Peter and Andrew would tell lots of people the good news about Jesus. Peter and Andrew and their partners pulled their boats up on the beach, left everything and followed Jesus.

Jesus heals Peter's mother-in-law.

Matthew 8:14,15;
Mark 1:29-31;
Luke 4:38,39

Jesus heals Peter's mother-in-law.

Matthew 8:14,15; Mark 1:29-31; Luke 4:38,39

Peter's wife's mother was sick. She lay in bed. Her head was hot. Her family felt afraid. They wanted her to get well.

Jesus and His friends went to Peter's house. Peter's family asked Jesus to help her get well. Jesus bent down and touched her hand. Right away she was well! She got up and helped to serve food to Jesus and His friends.

Jesus talks to Nicodemus about God's love.
John 3:1-21

Jesus talks to Nicodemus about God's love.

John 3:1-21

The Pharisees were people who thought they knew all about God. Most of the Pharisees didn't like Jesus. They were afraid people wouldn't pay any attention to them if Jesus kept teaching. Most of the Pharisees wanted to make Jesus stop teaching and healing people.

Nicodemus was a Pharisee. But Nicodemus wanted to learn more about Jesus. He went to see Jesus at night when no one else was around.

Jesus told Nicodemus that God loved everyone in the world so much that God sent His Son Jesus to die on the cross. Because of that, everyone who believes in Jesus can have eternal life with Jesus. Nicodemus didn't understand everything that Jesus said. Jesus explained that when people believe in Jesus, they are forgiven for the wrong things they do.

Jesus talks to a Samaritan woman.

John 4:1-42

Jesus talks to a Samaritan woman.

John 4:1-42

Jesus and His friends walked to the country of Samaria. It was a long walk. Jesus was tired, so He sat down by a well to rest. Jesus' friends went into town to find some food to eat.

While Jesus' friends were gone, a woman came to the well to get some water. It was very hot outside. The sun was very bright. The woman brought a big jar to fill with water. It must have been hard work to carry the heavy jar.

"May I have a drink?" Jesus asked. The woman was surprised! Men never talked to women in public places back then. Jesus told the woman some secrets she had. Jesus showed her that He cared about her. Jesus told her He was the Messiah—the Savior God promised to send. The woman went back to the town to tell others about Jesus. She brought many people back to see Jesus so they could hear Him, too.

Jesus calms a storm.

Matthew 8:23-27; Mark 4:35-41;
Luke 8:22-25

Jesus calms a storm.

Matthew 8:23-27; Mark 4:35-41; Luke 8:22-25

One night Jesus and His friends were sailing across the lake in their boat. Jesus was very tired. He lay down in the back of the boat. Soon He was asleep.

Suddenly, the wind began to blow. The wind blew harder and harder. The little waves got bigger and bigger. The big waves hit hard against the little boat. Water splashed into the boat. The boat was filling with water.

Jesus' friends were afraid. But Jesus slept quietly through the storm.

"Jesus! Help us!" shouted a friend. "Don't you care that our boat is sinking?"

Jesus woke up. Jesus stood up and said, "Quiet! Be still!" And just like that, the wind stopped blowing. The big waves stopped splashing.

"Why were you so afraid?" Jesus asked His friends. "Don't you know that I will take care of you?"

Jesus' friends were amazed that the winds and the waves had obeyed Jesus.

Jesus heals a paralyzed man.

Matthew 9:2-8; Mark 2:1-12; Luke 5:17-26

Jesus heals a paralyzed man.

Matthew 9:2-8; Mark 2:1-12; Luke 5:17-26

Many people came to hear Jesus teach. They crowded into the house. They even stood around the outside of the house. Some men came carrying their friend on a mat. Their friend couldn't move. He just had to lie on his mat.

The men wanted Jesus to help their friend, but they couldn't get through the crowd to bring their friend to Jesus. The men carried their friend up some stairs to the flat roof of the house. They dug a hole in the roof right over where Jesus was standing. They put ropes on their friend's mat. They carefully lowered the mat down in front of Jesus.

Jesus saw that the men believed in Him. Jesus told the man on the mat that his sins were forgiven. Then Jesus told him to get up. The man got up. He could walk! The crowd was amazed. They praised God!

A woman touches Jesus and is healed.

Matthew 9:20-22; Mark 5:25-34; Luke 8:43-48

A woman touches Jesus and is healed.

Matthew 9:20-22; Mark 5:25-34; Luke 8:43-48

There were many people all around Jesus. Everyone wanted to be close to Jesus. Everyone wanted to hear what He said. Everyone wanted to see what He did. Suddenly, Jesus asked, "Who touched me?"

Jesus' friends looked around. "There are many people here. We're all bumping into each other," they said.

"No," Jesus replied. "Someone touched me. I know that power has gone out from me."

A woman came and bowed before Jesus. "I touched you because I wanted to be healed. I have been sick for many years. As soon as I touched you, I could tell that I wasn't sick anymore!"

Jesus smiled and said, "Your faith has healed you. Go in peace."

Jesus heals Jairus's daughter.
Matthew 9:18-26; Mark 5:22-43; Luke 8:40-56

Jesus heals Jairus's daughter.

Matthew 9:18-26; Mark 5:22-43; Luke 8:40-56

Jairus's daughter was sick. Jairus went to see Jesus. "Please come and heal my daughter." Jesus went with Jairus. As they walked to Jairus's house, a helper came and said that Jairus's little girl was already dead.

Jesus said, "Don't be afraid. She will be fine." When they got to Jairus's house, Jesus told everyone to leave the little girl's room. Then Jesus and the little girl's parents went into the room.

Jesus took the little girl by the hand and said, "My child, get up!" Right away she stood up. Jesus told her parents to give her something to eat. Her parents were amazed to see Jesus' power over death.

Jesus uses a boy's lunch to feed 5,000 people.

Matthew 14:13-21; Mark 6:30-44; Luke 9:10-17; John 6:1-15

Jesus uses a boy's lunch to feed 5,000 people.

Matthew 14:13-21; Mark 6:30-44; Luke 9:10-17; John 6:1-15

Many people followed Jesus. They listened to Him talk all day long. They didn't have any food to eat and it was getting late. The people were hungry. They were a long way from a town with food.

Jesus told His friends to give the people something to eat. Jesus' friends didn't have enough food for all the people. Only one little boy had some food. It was just enough for one person to have lunch, but the little boy wanted to share his food.

Jesus told the people to sit down. Jesus took the boy's lunch and prayed. Then Jesus broke off pieces of bread and fish. His friends gave the food to the people. There was more than enough for everyone to eat. It was a miracle—something only God could do. One little boy's lunch became enough food for everyone to eat!

Jesus walks on the water and helps His friends.

Matthew 14:22-33; Mark 6:45-52; John 6:16-21

Jesus walks on the water and helps His friends.

Matthew 14:22-33; Mark 6:45-52; John 6:16-21

Jesus' friends were in a boat on the Sea of Galilee. The waves were coming over the side of the boat. The waves were very strong. Jesus' friends worked hard to row the boat.

Suddenly, Jesus' friends saw something that terrified them! They saw a man walking on the water. Jesus' friends knew that people couldn't walk on water. They thought they were seeing a ghost!

Jesus called out to them. "Don't be afraid," He said. "It's Me!" When Peter realized it was Jesus walking on the water, Peter wanted to walk out to Him. Jesus told Peter to come. Peter started to walk on the water to Jesus. When Peter looked at the waves, he was afraid and started to sink. Jesus took Peter by the hand and pulled him up. They got into the boat, and at once the sea was still.

Jesus heals a man who couldn't hear or talk.

Mark 7:31-37

Jesus heals a man who couldn't hear or talk.

Mark 7:31-37

Some people brought to Jesus a man who couldn't hear or talk. "Please make this man well," they said.

Jesus walked a little way away with the man. Jesus didn't want everyone in the crowd that was following Him to listen when He talked to the man.

Jesus put His fingers into the man's ears. Then Jesus spit and touched the man's tongue. Jesus looked up to heaven. He said, "Be opened!" As soon as Jesus said this, the man could hear and he could talk plainly.

Jesus told the man and his friends not to tell others what had happened, but they were so amazed that they just kept on talking about the wonderful thing Jesus did.

Only one man says thank-you to Jesus.

Luke 17:11-19

Only one man says thank-you to Jesus.

Luke 17:11-19

Jesus and His friends were walking. As they came near a village, Some men saw Jesus. These ten men had a disease called leprosy. The ten men didn't run to Jesus because people who had leprosy had to stay away from everyone! That was the law. So the men with leprosy called out to Jesus. They said, "Jesus, have pity on us!"

When Jesus saw and heard the men, He told them to go and show themselves to the priests. As the ten men walked to the priests, they saw that they were cured. None of them had leprosy anymore!

One of the ten men turned around and ran back to Jesus. He started to praise God in a loud voice. Other people must have heard him. Other people must have been excited to see him healthy instead of sick. The man thanked Jesus for healing him.

Jesus said, "Didn't I heal ten men? Where are the other nine?" Then Jesus said to the man who came back, "Get up and go. Your faith has made you well." The healed man was very happy!

Jesus loves the children.

Matthew 19:13-15; Mark 10:13-16; Luke 18:15-17

Jesus loves the children.

Matthew 19:13-15; Mark 10:13-16; Luke 18:15-17

One day Jesus was teaching His friends and other people about God. They were listening carefully to what Jesus was saying. Just then, a group of people came to see Jesus.

Jesus and His friends looked at these people and saw that it was children and their parents. The children and their mothers and fathers were so excited to see Jesus.

But when they came near to Jesus, His friends thought that Jesus was too busy to talk to the children. Jesus' friends said, "Don't bring those children here!" The children and their parents were sad to hear those words. They started to walk away.

But wait! Jesus said, "Let the children come to Me! I want to see them!" Jesus was not too busy to see the children! Jesus loved them!

Right away, the children ran to Jesus. They crowded close to Him. Some even climbed up on His lap. Jesus put His arms around them. What a happy day! The children knew Jesus loved them!

Jesus helps a blind man see.

John 9:1-41

Jesus helps a blind man see.

John 9:1-41

One day Jesus saw a man who had been blind his whole life. The man had never seen grass or the sky or his mom's face. Jesus took some dirt, spit in it and made some mud. Then Jesus put the mud on the man's eyes. Jesus told the man to wash his eyes in a pool of water. The man went and washed his eyes just like Jesus said. Then the man could see!

When the man got home, many people were amazed. Some people asked, "Isn't this the same man who used to sit and beg?"

Others said, "No, he only looks like the blind man."

But the man born blind said, "I am the one. Jesus made some mud and put it on my eyes. Then Jesus told me to go and wash my eyes in a pool of water. So I did and now I can see."

Jesus tells about a good Samaritan.

Luke 10:25-37

Jesus tells about a good Samaritan.

Luke 10:25-37

Jesus told this story: A man was going from Jerusalem to Jericho, when he got hurt by some robbers. The robbers took everything the man had and beat him up. Then they went away, leaving him hurt and almost dead.

A priest happened to be walking down the same road. When he saw the man, he passed by on the other side of the road. A Levite (a helper in the Temple) also walked by and saw the hurt man. The Levite didn't help the man either. But then, a Samaritan man came to where the man was. The Samaritan saw that the man was Jewish. He knew that Jews and Samaritans did not like each other. But the Samaritan stopped to help. He bandaged the hurt man's sores and put the man on his own donkey. The Samaritan took him to an inn. He even paid the innkeeper to take care of the hurt man!

Jesus asked, "Who was a neighbor to the man who got hurt?" The one who was a neighbor was the one who helped the hurt man. Jesus wants everyone to help others the same way.

Mary listens to Jesus.
Luke 10:38-42

Mary listens to Jesus.

Luke 10:38-42

Jesus and His friends came to a town called Bethany. A woman named Martha and her sister Mary lived there. They invited Jesus to come to their home. Martha worked hard to prepare a good dinner for Jesus. She cooked and she cleaned. She noticed that her sister Mary was not helping!

Mary was sitting on the floor by Jesus' feet, listening to everything that Jesus was saying. Martha was not happy. There was work to do and Mary wasn't helping her! Finally Martha said to Jesus, "Don't you care that my sister has left me to do the work by myself? Tell her to help me!"

Jesus just said, "Martha, Martha, you are worried and upset about many things. Mary chose to listen to me. That is more important than all those other things."

Jesus tells about a patient father.

Luke 15:11-32

Jesus tells about a patient father.

Luke 15:11-32

Jesus told a story about a man and his two sons. The younger son asked his father for the money that he would one day inherit. The father gave the son what the son wanted.

Soon after that, the younger son took all his money and went to another country. He spent all his money on parties and buying things for his friends. After his money was gone there was a famine. There was no food for him to eat! None of his friends would help him. The only work he could find was feeding pigs. He was so hungry that he wanted to eat the food the pigs were eating!

Finally the son realized what he should do. He decided to go back home and ask to be hired as one of his father's servants. When the son was still far away, his father saw him. His father ran to him and threw his arms around him.

The son said, "Father, I was wrong. I'm not good enough to be called your son." But the father called to his servants. "Bring some new clothes for my son," he said. "Get ready for a party! My son has come home!"

Zaccheus climbs a tree to see Jesus.

Luke 19:1-9

Zacchaeus climbs a tree to see Jesus.

Luke 19:1-9

Many people followed Jesus. They wanted to see what He did and hear what He said. There were so many people that Zacchaeus couldn't see. He stood on his tiptoes, but he still couldn't see. He jumped up and down, but the other people were too tall. He asked taller people to move over, but they ignored him. Zacchaeus was too short. And nobody would help him because Zacchaeus had cheated them all out of a lot of money.

Finally, Zacchaeus ran ahead of the crowd. Zacchaeus found a tree that he knew Jesus would pass by. Zacchaeus climbed the tree and waited.

The crowd came closer. Now Zacchaeus could see Jesus! Jesus was coming toward the tree! Jesus stopped under the tree. Jesus looked up at Zacchaeus and said, "Zacchaeus, come down. I must stay at your house today." Zacchaeus was excited!

Zacchaeus climbed down the tree and hurried home with Jesus. Zacchaeus wanted to do what was right. He gave half of everything he had to the poor. He promised to give back four times anything he had stolen. Zacchaeus was glad Jesus loved him.

Jesus brings Lazarus back to life.

John 11:1-44

Bible Story Coloring Pages • 187

Jesus brings Lazarus back to life.

John 11:1-44

Some men ran to Jesus. "Your friend, Lazarus, is very sick. Please come and heal him." Jesus wanted to help Lazarus. But instead of going right away to see Lazarus, Jesus waited. Then Jesus told His friends, "Let's go see Lazarus."

Jesus and His friends walked a long way. They finally got to the place where Lazarus lived. Lazarus's sister Martha went out to meet Jesus.

"Oh, Jesus," she said, "if you had been here my brother would not have died!" Martha, her sister Mary and many other people were so sad because Lazarus had died. Many of them were crying. Jesus saw all the sad people and He started to cry too.

Jesus and all the people went to the tomb where they put Lazarus's body. Jesus said, "Take away the stone."

Jesus prayed. Then Jesus said, "Lazarus, come out!" Lazarus came out of the tomb. Lazarus wasn't dead anymore! He was alive because Jesus raised him from the dead!

People welcome Jesus to Jerusalem.

Matthew 21:1-11; Mark 11:1-11; Luke 19:28-44

People welcome Jesus to Jerusalem.

Matthew 21:1-11; Mark 11:1-11; Luke 19:28-44

What a happy day! Jesus and His friends were going to the Temple in Jerusalem. On the way, Jesus stopped. He said to His friends, "There is a little donkey in the town. Untie it and bring it to Me."

Jesus climbed onto the donkey's back and began riding to the city. Many other people were walking along the road to Jerusalem. Some people were so happy to see Jesus that they spread their coats on the road. Other people cut branches from palm trees and laid them on the road for Jesus' donkey to walk on. They were treating Jesus like a king!

Some people ran ahead to tell others, "Jesus is coming!" And even more people came to see Jesus. They said, "Hosanna! Hosanna!" (That means "Save us.") It was a wonderful day in Jerusalem! The people praised Jesus!

Jesus clears the Temple.
Matthew 21:12-16; Mark 11:12-19; Luke 19:45-48

Jesus clears the Temple.

Matthew 21:12-16; Mark 11:12-19; Luke 19:45-48

Jesus went to the Temple. The Temple was a special place for talking to God and learning about Him. But there were people in the Temple who were making noise selling things.

"Doves for sale!" someone shouted.

"Buy your lambs over here!" Someone else called. They were charging too much and cheating the people. The sellers were so loud that people who wanted to pray couldn't. No one could talk to God or learn about Him when people were yelling like that.

When Jesus saw this, He was angry. Jesus forced the sellers to leave the Temple. Then sick people came to Jesus. Jesus healed them and talked to the people about God.

**A poor woman
gives all she has.**

Mark 12:41-44; Luke 21:1-4

A poor woman gives all she has.

Mark 12:41-44; Luke 21:1-4

Jesus and His friends were sitting by the Temple. Many people came by to give money to God at the Temple. They walked up to a big metal box and dropped their money inside. CLANG! CLANG! The money made lots of noise. Some rich people put in lots of money. The money banged and clanged and everyone looked at the rich people.

Then a poor woman went to the box. She only had two tiny coins. She very quietly dropped her tiny coins into the box. Her money didn't make any noise. No one turned and looked. But Jesus saw what she did. "This woman has given more than any of the rich people," Jesus told His friends. "The others just gave some of their money. She gave all her money."

A woman shows love to Jesus.
Matthew 26:6-13; Mark 14:3-9; John 12:2-8

A woman shows love to Jesus.

Matthew 26:6-13; Mark 14:3-9; John 12:2-8

Jesus and some of His friends were having dinner at Simon's house. A woman came into the room holding a jar of very expensive perfume. The woman opened the jar and poured the perfume on Jesus' head and feet. The wonderful smell of the perfume filled the house.

Some of Jesus' friends were not happy. "Why did she waste this expensive perfume?" they said. "She could have sold it and given the money to the poor."

Jesus said, "Don't bother her. She has done a beautiful thing. You can always give to the poor, but I won't always be here like this." Jesus was glad the woman had shown how much she loved Him.

Jesus washes His friends' feet.

John 13:1-17

Jesus washes His friends' feet.

John 13:1-17

Jesus and His friends were getting ready to have a special dinner together. They spent the day talking and walking. The roads were hot and dusty.

When Jesus and His friends came to the house for a special dinner, their feet were dirty. They needed to be washed! But no one wanted to wash other people's feet. That was a job for a servant!

Jesus waited until the food was on the table. Then Jesus got up and wrapped a towel around His waist. Jesus poured water into a large bowl and began to wash His friends' feet.

Peter felt embarrassed. Peter knew that he should have offered to wash Jesus' feet. But Jesus told Peter that he needed Jesus to wash his feet for him.

"Follow my example," Jesus said. He wanted them to help each other.

Jesus eats a special meal with His friends.

Matthew 26:17-30; Mark 14:12-26; Luke 22:7-38

Jesus eats a special meal with His friends.

Matthew 26:17-30; Mark 14:12-26; Luke 22:7-38

Jesus and His friends were in Jerusalem to celebrate a holiday together. The holiday was called the Passover. Jewish people celebrate the Passover every year to remind them of the time God freed them from slavery.

As part of the holiday, Jesus and His friends ate a special meal. Jesus picked up some bread from the table. Jesus said thank-you to God for the bread. Then Jesus broke the bread into pieces and gave some bread to each of His friends.

"Take and eat. This is my body given for you," Jesus said. He compared the bread to His body.

Then Jesus took a cup and thanked God for it. "Drink from this cup. This is my blood shed for many people," Jesus said. Jesus gave the cup to each friend.

The bread and the cup were reminders of what was going to happen soon: Jesus' death on the cross. This special meal, called the Last Supper, reminds everyone who follows Jesus of His love and God's plan to forgive sins.

Peter lies about knowing Jesus.

Matthew 26:69-75; Mark 14:66-72;
Luke 22:55-62; John 18:15-18,25-27

Peter lies about knowing Jesus.

Matthew 26:69-75; Mark 14:66-72;
Luke 22:55-62; John 18:15-18,25-27

Jesus had been arrested by people who wanted to hurt Him. Peter was scared. He was afraid he might be arrested, too. A servant girl asked Peter if he was one of Jesus' friends. Peter lied. "I don't know what you are talking about," he said. The servant girl told some other people that she thought Peter was one of Jesus' friends. Peter got angry and said, "I don't know Him!"

Later on some other people said, "You must be one of Jesus' friends." Peter was still afraid and said, "I don't know the man!" Right away a rooster began to crow.

Suddenly Peter remembered Jesus' words. Jesus had said that Peter would lie about Him three times before a rooster crowed in the morning. Peter didn't want to lie about Jesus because Peter loved Jesus very much. Peter was very sorry that he had lied about Jesus. Peter went outside and cried. Later, Jesus showed that He still loved Peter, and He forgave Peter.

Jesus dies on the cross.

Matthew 27:32-56; Mark 15:21-41;
Luke 23:26-49; John 19:17-37

Jesus dies on the cross.

Matthew 27:32-56; Mark 15:21-41;
Luke 23:26-49; John 19:17-37

One day, Jesus told His friends, "In a few days, some people are going to take Me away. I'm going to be killed." Jesus' friends were sad. Jesus knew this was part of God's plan so people could be forgiven for wrong things they have done. And Jesus knew He wouldn't stay dead!

The people who wanted to kill Jesus did not like it that so many people loved Him. When these people came to get Jesus, Jesus let them take Him. And He let them kill Him on a cross.

Jesus' friends were sad. They took Jesus' body and put it into a tomb. A tomb was a little room cut out of the side of a hill. Some men put a huge rock in front of the doorway of the tomb. Jesus' friends were very sad. They didn't know that something wonderful was going to happen.

Jesus talks to Mary in the garden.

John 20:10-18

Jesus talks to Mary in the garden.

John 20:10-18

Mary felt very sad. She thought she would never see Jesus again. Mary went to the tomb where Jesus' body was. Mary wanted to put some spices on Jesus' body (as people did in Bible times when someone died).

When Mary got to the tomb, she saw that it was empty! Jesus' body wasn't there anymore. Mary cried and cried. She didn't know that Jesus was alive. Mary saw two angels. They asked, "Why are you crying?"

Mary said, "Someone has taken Jesus' body and I don't know where they have put it." Then Mary turned around and saw a man standing there.

"Woman," the man said, "why are you crying? Who are you looking for?" Mary thought that He was a gardener.

Mary said, "Sir, if you have taken him away, tell me where you have put him."

The man just said her name, "Mary." Right away Mary knew that He was Jesus and He was alive! Mary felt so happy! Jesus told Mary to go and tell His friends that He was alive.

Jesus talks to His friends.

Mark 16:14; Luke 24:36-43; John 20:19-23

Jesus talks to His friends.

Mark 16:14; Luke 24:36-43; John 20:19-23

Most of Jesus' special friends were together in a room with the doors locked. They were afraid that the people who killed Jesus would try to hurt them, too.

Suddenly Jesus was in the room with them! He didn't come through the door—it was locked. He didn't come through the windows—they were shut. He just appeared!

Jesus said, "Peace be with you." His friends were afraid! They thought Jesus was a ghost. "Why are you afraid?" Jesus asked. "Why don't you believe that it is really me? Touch me and see that I am really alive. I'm not a ghost." Jesus showed them His hands and His feet that still had marks from when He was on the cross. Jesus even ate some fish with them. Jesus explained to them that He had to die on the cross so that people everywhere could have their sins forgiven. Finally, the friends believed that Jesus really was alive. They were so happy!

Thomas believes when he sees Jesus.

John 20:24-29

Thomas believes when he sees Jesus.

John 20:24-29

Some of Jesus' friends were excited! "We have seen Jesus!" Jesus' friends said. "He is alive!"

Thomas was sad. Thomas knew that Jesus had died. Thomas didn't believe that Jesus had come back to life. "I won't believe that Jesus is alive unless I see Him and touch Him," Thomas said.

Later Thomas and Jesus' other friends were together in a house. The doors were locked so that no one could get in. Suddenly, Jesus appeared in the room. Jesus knew that Thomas still didn't believe He was really alive. Jesus must have smiled at Thomas. "Come and touch Me, Thomas," Jesus said. "I want you to know that I am alive." Thomas was glad to see Jesus! Now Thomas knew for sure that Jesus was alive.

Jesus cooks breakfast on the beach.
John 21:1-25

Jesus cooks breakfast on the beach.

John 21:1-25

After Jesus died and came back to life, some of Jesus' friends went fishing. They fished all night long, but didn't catch any fish. They were still in their boats on the lake when morning came. As it got light, they could see someone standing on the beach. He called out, "Do you have any fish?"

Jesus' friends answered, "No."

"Throw your net on the right side of the boat and you will find some fish," the man said. When Jesus' friends threw out the net, they caught so many fish that they couldn't pull the net back onto the boat. Peter knew it was Jesus talking to them! Peter jumped into the water and swam to the beach to see Jesus. The others followed in the boat. They towed the net full of fish behind them.

When they got to the shore, they saw that Jesus was cooking breakfast. There was a fire with some fish on it and some bread. Jesus invited them to have breakfast with Him.

Jesus goes back to heaven.

Luke 24:50-53; Acts 1:1-11

• Bible Story Coloring Pages • 213

Jesus goes back to heaven.

Luke 24:50-53; Acts 1:1-11

After Jesus came back to life, He spent many days talking to His friends. One day they went to the top of a hill. "Tell people all over the world about Me," Jesus said. Jesus promised that the Holy Spirit would come and make them able to do everything Jesus asked them to do.

Then Jesus went up to heaven. Jesus' friends watched as Jesus went up in the air. Soon Jesus was covered up by clouds. Jesus' friends couldn't see Him anymore, but they kept looking up for a while.

Suddenly two angels stood beside them. "Why do you stand here looking into the sky?" They asked. "Jesus will come back someday the same way you saw Him go up into heaven." Then Jesus' friends went to Jerusalem to pray and wait for the Holy Spirit to come.

God sends the Holy Spirit.

Acts 2:1-13

God sends the Holy Spirit.

Acts 2:1-13

After Jesus went back to heaven, His friends prayed and stayed together in Jerusalem. One morning, a sound like a strong wind blowing filled the house where they were staying. Something that looked like a small fire sat on top of each person's head! The Holy Spirit Jesus promised had finally come!

There were people from many different places staying in Jerusalem. These people spoke many different languages. When they heard the noise, they gathered around the house to see what was going on.

Jesus' friends began to speak in other languages, telling all the people about Jesus. The people in Jerusalem were amazed because they heard what Jesus' friends were saying about Jesus in their own languages! Many people believed in Jesus and started to tell other people about Jesus, too.

Barnabas shows his love for Jesus by sharing.
Acts 4:32-37

Barnabas shows his love for Jesus by sharing.

Acts 4:32-37

One of the ways Jesus' friends showed their love was by sharing everything they had.

Some people had lots of food and clothing. But they didn't keep it all for themselves. They shared their food and clothes with people who had no food and clothing. If a family had more food than they needed, they gave it to people who did not have enough food.

One of Jesus' friends who shared was a man named Barnabas. He was a cheerful, happy man. He helped other people so much that his friends gave him a nickname. His nickname meant something like "Mr. Helper."

Barnabas owned a field. He could have kept it for himself. But instead, Barnabas sold the land. Barnabas could have spent that money. But Barnabas took the money to the leaders of Jesus' followers. He said, "Here, share this money with people who need it."

Barnabas wanted to do what was right. So Barnabas showed he loved Jesus by sharing with other people.

Philip tells the good news about Jesus to an Ethiopian man.

Acts 8:26-40

Philip tells the good news about Jesus to an Ethiopian man.

Acts 8:26-40

An angel told Philip to walk on a certain road in the desert. Philip did what the angel said. As he walked, Philip saw a man riding in a chariot. This man worked for the queen of Ethiopia. He was reading a scroll with words from the Bible.

God told Philip to go to the man's chariot and stay with it. Philip had to run to catch up with the chariot. Philip heard the man reading words from the Bible. Philip asked the man if he understood what he was reading. The Ethiopian man said, "How can I unless someone explains it to me?" The man invited Philip to ride with him in the chariot.

Philip explained that the words the man was reading told about Jesus. Philip told the man that Jesus died and came back to life again so people who believe in Jesus can live forever with Him. When they came to some water, the man stopped the chariot. To show that he believed in Jesus, Philip baptized him. Then Philip disappeared! God took Philip to another place. The Ethiopian man went back home happy because he knew Jesus.

Jesus talks to Saul.

Acts 9:1-19

Jesus talks to Saul.

Acts 9:1-19

Saul was certain that Jesus' friends were telling lies. Saul didn't believe that Jesus was God's Son. Saul wanted to make people stop talking about Jesus. Saul was so angry that he even wanted to kill people who believed in Jesus!

Saul went to Damascus to find people who believed in Jesus and take them as prisoners to Jerusalem. As he walked along the road with some friends, a bright light suddenly flashed around Saul. Saul fell to the ground. Jesus talked to Saul. "Why are you hurting me?" Jesus said. "Go to Damascus and you will be told what you must do." Saul got up, but he could not see. Saul's friends helped Saul walk to Damascus.

For three days, Saul was blind and he didn't eat anything. He prayed to God. God sent a man who loved Jesus to help Saul. The man went to the house where Saul was staying and said, "The Lord Jesus sent me so that you may see again." Right away, Saul could see. Now Saul loved and obeyed Jesus.

Saul escapes in a basket. Acts 9:19-25

Saul escapes in a basket.

Acts 9:19-25

Saul was telling the good news about Jesus. Many people were surprised because Saul used to hate people who loved Jesus. Saul used to put people who worshiped Jesus in jail. But now Saul loved Jesus too, and he wanted other people to know about Jesus. Saul told many people that Jesus was really God's Son.

Some people were angry that Saul was preaching about Jesus. They made a plan to kill Saul. They waited by the gates to the city. They wanted to catch Saul going somewhere by himself. Then they could kill him!

Some of Saul's new friends found out about the plan to hurt Saul. In the middle of the night, Saul's friends put Saul in a big basket and lowered it down over the wall. Saul escaped from the people who wanted to kill him!

God brings Dorcas to life again after Peter prays.

Acts 9:32-43

God brings Dorcas to life again after Peter prays.

Acts 9:32-43

Dorcas loved to help other people. She made clothes for others. She always helped the poor. She always tried to do good things. All the people in her town really loved her.

But Dorcas got very sick, so sick that she died. Her friends were very sad. Some of Dorcas's friends heard that Peter, Jesus' friend, was in a nearby town. They went to see Peter, and asked him to come to see Dorcas.

Peter came. Dorcas's friends took him to the room where Dorcas was. Peter told them all to leave the room. Peter got down on his knees and prayed. Then Peter looked at Dorcas and said, "Dorcas, get up." She opened her eyes and sat up. Peter helped her up and led her downstairs to where her friends were waiting. She was alive! Many people in Dorcas's town believed in Jesus because God made Dorcas alive.

Peter preaches to Cornelius.
Acts 10:1-48

Peter preaches to Cornelius.

Acts 10:1-48

Cornelius was a Roman soldier. He tried to do what was right and serve God. But he didn't know about Jesus. God sent an angel to talk to Cornelius. "Send some men to get Peter to come and talk to you," the angel said. Cornelius did what the angel said.

Just before Cornelius's men got to the house where Peter was staying, Peter was on the roof waiting for lunch to be ready. Peter started to pray. While he was praying, God showed him in a dream that God loves all people. God told Peter to go with the men who were coming to see him.

Soon the men came to Peter's house. Peter went downstairs to greet the men. "Why are you looking for me?" he asked. The men told Peter about how an angel had spoken to Cornelius. Peter invited the men into the house and gave them some food to eat. The next morning Peter went with them to Cornelius's house. Peter told everyone there about Jesus. Cornelius and all his family believed and were baptized.

An angel frees Peter.

Acts 12:1-19

An angel frees Peter.

Acts 12:1-19

King Herod put Peter in prison. He decided to kill Peter because some angry men did not want Peter to keep preaching about Jesus. That night Peter slept chained to two guards in his prison cell. More guards stood at the entrance. They didn't want Peter to escape!

Suddenly an angel appeared in Peter's prison cell. The angel said, "Quick, get up!" The chains fell right off Peter's wrists. Then the angel told Peter to get dressed and follow him. They walked out of the prison, right past the guards. The gate to the city even opened by itself to let them in! Then the angel disappeared!

Peter quickly went to a house where some other believers in Jesus were praying for him. Peter knocked on the door. The servant girl who came to the door was so surprised that she forgot to open the door and let him in! When Peter finally was let into the house, he explained to everyone what had happened. They all praised God together for answering their prayers and rescuing Peter.

Lydia believes in Jesus.

Acts 16:11-15

Lydia believes in Jesus.

Acts 16:11-15

Paul (who used to be called Saul) and some others traveled to another city. They looked for people who loved God and wanted to learn more about Him. Some women were sitting by the river. The women gathered there to pray and talk about God. Paul and the others sat down with the women to talk to them about Jesus.

"Jesus is God's Son," they said. "He died and came back to life again so that you can live forever with Him." Lydia heard what Paul and the others said. Lydia believed what they said. Lydia loved God. Her whole family believed in Jesus when they heard about Him.

"Come and stay at my house," Lydia said. Paul and the other believers stayed with Lydia for a while.

**Paul and Silas sing
praise to God in jail.**

Acts 16:16-40

Paul and Silas sing praise to God in jail.

Acts 16:16-40

Paul and his friend Silas were put in jail because some people were angry with them. The jailer put chains on their feet. Paul and Silas didn't act afraid.

Paul and Silas sang songs and prayed to God. The other prisoners in the jail listened to Paul and Silas.

In the middle of the night, the ground began to shake and the walls of the jail began to crumble. There was a terrible earthquake and all the doors of the jail came open. The chains on Paul and Silas came off!

The jailer thought that all the prisoners had escaped. The jailer decided that it would be better to kill himself than to be punished for losing the prisoners.

Paul cried out, "Don't hurt yourself! We are all still here!" The jailer took Paul and Silas out of the jail and took them home to take care of them. Now the jailer wanted to know about Jesus. Everyone in the jailer's family heard the good news about Jesus and believed in Him.

Paul tells a king about Jesus.
Acts 25:13—26:32

Paul tells a king about Jesus.

Acts 25:13—26:32

One day soldiers brought Paul to a big city. Paul was put in jail there because some people did not want Paul to talk about Jesus. These people asked the governor to keep Paul in jail. The governor's name was Festus.

While Paul was in jail, a king and his wife came to visit Festus. Festus told them about Paul. "Let me hear this man Paul," the king said to Festus.

"All right," Festus said. "I will have Paul come from jail tomorrow so you can hear him talk."

The very next day, the soldiers brought Paul from the jail. Paul was glad he could tell the good news about Jesus. "Jesus is God's Son," Paul said. Paul told them many other things about Jesus, too.

Festus didn't understand what Paul was saying. "Paul, you're crazy," Festus shouted.

Paul answered, "I am not crazy. What I am saying is true. I pray that you will believe Jesus is God's Son, just as I do."

Paul's ship wrecks in a storm.

Acts 27:1-44

Paul's ship wrecks in a storm.

Acts 27:1-44

Paul and many other people climbed onto a big ship. Paul knew it would not be safe to travel on the sea at this time. He told the people on the ship, "If we sail now, we'll have problems." The people didn't listen. The wind began to blow. It blew the ship out to sea.

Then the wind began to blow harder and harder. Splash! Splash! The waves splashed high in the air and into the ship. The waves almost knocked the ship over! Big dark clouds covered the sky. Rain came pouring down. Everyone on the ship was afraid.

Paul had good news for the people. "Don't be afraid," Paul said. "No one will be hurt. God sent an angel to tell me that God will take care of all of us."

Early in the morning, the people saw land! They tried to sail to the shore. But the big, strong waves pushed the ship into some sand just under the water. Crash! The ship broke apart into little pieces. All the people jumped into the water. They found their way to the land. No one had been hurt. God took care of all the people.

A snake bites Paul.

Acts 28:1-6

A snake bites Paul.

Acts 28:1-6

Paul and all the people on the ship were safe after their ship broke apart. They swam or floated on pieces of their ship to an island called Malta.

The people who lived on the island built a fire and helped take care of all the people from the ship. Paul helped to build the fire, too. Paul picked up some wood to put on the fire. When he put the wood on the fire, a snake came out of the wood and bit Paul on the hand.

The people on the island knew this snake was dangerous. They thought that the snake's bite would make Paul die. But God didn't let Paul die. The snake bite didn't hurt Paul. The people on the island were amazed.

Paul writes letters to help others follow Jesus.
2 Timothy 1:1—4:22

Paul writes letters to help others follow Jesus.

2 Timothy 1:1—4:22

Paul wrote many letters to different churches and to different people. Paul wanted to tell others about Jesus. He wanted to help people who loved Jesus know the right things to do. Sometimes Paul wrote letters while he was on a trip. Sometimes he even wrote letters when he was in prison!

Paul wasn't put in prison because he did anything wrong. Paul was put in prison several times because some people didn't want him to tell other people about Jesus.

One time Paul was in a deep, dark dungeon. He wrote a letter to Timothy. Timothy was Paul's friend. Paul wanted to tell Timothy many things. Paul also wanted Timothy to come and visit him in prison. Paul helped Timothy learn how to live as a follower of Jesus.

Paul sends Onesimus home.

Philemon 1-25

Paul sends Onesimus home.

Philemon 1-25

Onesimus was in trouble! He had run away. He had taken things with him that weren't his. The things he had taken belonged to Philemon, the man Onesimus had run away from.

One day Onesimus met Paul, a man who loved Jesus. Paul wanted to help Onesimus. Paul told Onesimus about Jesus. Soon Onesimus loved Jesus, too.

Onesimus knew it had been wrong to take things that belonged to Philemon. Onesimus knew he needed to go back to Philemon and say that he was sorry.

Paul wanted to help Onesimus. So he wrote a letter to Philemon. Paul wrote:

> *Dear Philemon,*
> *I am sending Onesimus, whom I love, back to you.*
> *Please welcome him as you would welcome me.*
> *If he owes you anything, charge it to me.*
> *Your friend, Paul.*

Paul gave the letter to Onesimus. Then he said, "You must go back to Philemon. Tell him you are sorry for the wrong things you have done."

John writes good news.
Revelation 1:1,2,9-11; 21:3-5

John writes good news.

Revelation 1:1,2,9-11; 21:3-5

When Jesus lived on earth, John was one of Jesus' best friends. One day Jesus went back to live with God in heaven. Then John told many people the good news that Jesus loves all people. But some people did not love Jesus. They did not like John, either. They took John away from his home and made him live on a lonely island.

John had to stay on the island a long, long time. Every day he thought about Jesus and prayed. One day when John was praying, something very special happened. John heard a voice say, "Write a book about the things you see. Then send the book to the people who love Me." John knew it was Jesus speaking to him!

Then Jesus showed John what heaven is like. He also showed John some things that will happen later. Jesus is going to come back! People who love Jesus will live with Him forever.

For many, many days John carefully wrote Jesus' words on special books called scrolls. In our Bible we can read the words about heaven that Jesus told John to write.

Smart Sunday School Helps
from Gospel Light

Grow Your Own Sunday School.

A ton of reproducible resources to help you recruit and motivate leaders and teachers, promote support within the congregation and increase attendance at Sunday School.

Sunday School Promo Pages
By Wes and Sheryl Haystead
Manual • ISBN 08307.15894

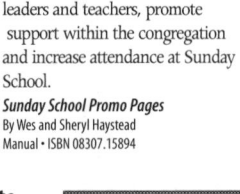

Hundreds of Bright Ideas for Children's Workers.

Advice, answers and articles on every aspect of teaching children. Reproducible so that you can give training to all of your teachers, volunteers and parents.

Sunday School Smart Pages
Edited by Wes and Sheryl Haystead
Manual • ISBN 08307.15215

Bible Skits for All Occasions.

52 lively reproducible Bible-theme skits in each book. Each skit includes director's tips, Bible background information and group discussion questions. Less than 33¢ per skit!

The Bible Skit Book
Manual • ISBN 08307.16238
More Bible Skits
Manual • ISBN 08307.16645

Here's a Colorful Way to Bring the Bible to Life!

Here's a great way to introduce Bible learning while the kids are busy with their crayons. *Bible Verse Coloring Pages* includes 116 verses in both NIV and KJV translations. These reproducible pages can be used again and again.

Bible Verse Coloring Pages
Coloring Book • SPCN 25116.06720

Hundreds of Smart Ideas for 5th and 6th Grade Sunday School.

Here's a life-saving resource that puts the most current articles, tips, and quick solutions for teaching 5th and 6th graders at your fingertips. Use these reproducible pages for on-the-spot training or teacher refreshment. The perfect companion for any brand of curriculum.

5th & 6th Grade Smart Pages
Manual • ISBN 08307.18052

Holiday Programming Just Got Easier!

Take the anxiety out of planning, staging and presenting programs for Advent, Christmas, Easter, Thanksgiving, Mother's Day and more. Includes 23 wide variety skits for all ages. Reproducible.

Holiday Skits
Manual • ISBN 08307.17781

Fun Games that Teach Kids About the Bible.

200 reproducible Bible learning games at your fingertips. Fun, active games for 1st through 6th graders that will help you review Bible stories, reinforce Bible memory verses and apply them to a child's life.

Big Book of Bible Games
Manual • ISBN 08307.18214

Give Your Kids the Best Parties!

With this easy-to-use resource you'll be able to plan and put on the best parties for your kids! Get decorating ideas, clip art, fun snack recipes, great games and activities and much more! This resource works with all children's programs, including special events, day camps, Sunday School, VBS, Christian schools and home birthday parties.

The Big Book of Theme Parties, Snacks and Games
Manual • ISBN 08307.18206

Bible Memory Music Kids from Six to Sixty Will Love.

Every word of these upbeat songs is straight from the Bible. It's the ultra-cool way to memorize the scriptures being studied in Gospel Light's 5th and 6th grade Sunday School curriculum, Planet 56! And it's reproducible–so you can make copies for all your kids.

The Bible in Your Brain Scripture Memory Music
Reproducible Cassette • SPCN 25116.09584
Reproducible CD • SPCN 25116.10264

Instant Art for Your Church.

These popular books include Bible verses, borders and hundreds of reproducible illustrations to help you create professional bulletins, flyers, posters and more. Complete with simple instructions.

Big Picture Bible Time Line
ISBN 08307.14723
Complete Bible Story Clip Art Book
ISBN 08307.13859
Sunday School Clip Art Book
ISBN 08307.11147

Make Any Bible Lesson Come to Life!

Hand puppets grab your kids attention and help them remember your lesson. Use them at home, in Sunday School, VBS and anytime you want a child's full attention. *Easy-to-Make Puppets and How to Use Them* gives you great ideas to use puppets in the classroom and at home. Includes reproducible patterns and guidelines to make your job easier.

Lofty the Bird Puppet
Hand Puppet • UPC 607135.001522
Paka the Lion Puppet
Hand Puppet • SPCN 25116.09029
Easy-to-Make Puppets and How to Use Them
Manual • ISBN 08307.16793

Craft Ideas for Creative Lessons.

Crafts make ideal teaching activities. Each of these crafts include step-by-step instructions, illustrations and patterns using economical and easy-to-find materials.

High Adventure Crafts for Kids
ISBN 08307.18516
Celebrating Our Families–Crafts for Kids
ISBN 08307.16750
Safari Crafts for Kids
ISBN 08307.17684
Bible Times Crafts for Kids
ISBN 08307.15967
Mountain Crafts for Kids
ISBN 08307.14766
Pioneer Crafts for Kids
ISBN 08307.14235
Country Crafts for Kids
ISBN 08307.16106
Handcraft Encyclopedia
ISBN 08307.14901
202 Things to Do
ISBN 08307.00269

Best-selling Clip Art You Can Use on Your Computer.

Bible Story Clip Art on disk
Windows • SPCN 25116.08952
Macintosh • SPCN 25116.08944
Kid's Worker's Clip Art on disk
Windows • SPCN 25116.06658
Macintosh • SPCN 25116.06631
Sunday School Clip Art on disk
Windows • SPCN 25116.08979
Macintosh • SPCN 25116.08960
Summer Ministries Clip Art on disk
Windows • SPCN 25116.10248
Macintosh • SPCN 25116.10221
Church Bulletin Clip Art on disk
Windows • SPCN 25116.06674
Macintosh • SPCN 25116.06666

Keep Track of Kids with Attendance Resources.

These resources make record keeping simple and efficient. Each large, colorful Attendance Chart lets you keep track of your students for over two months. Give kids Peel 'n Press stickers so they can measure their weekly attendance!

Hot-Air Balloon Theme Attendance Chart
SPCN 25116.09916
Farm Theme Attendance Chart
SPCN 25116.05279
Island Theme Attendance Chart
SPCN 25116.04868
Mountain Theme Attendance Chart
SPCN 25116.02172
Pioneer Theme Attendance Chart
SPCN 25116.04876
Attendance Cards
SPCN 25116.02806 (Pack of 100)

Class Record Book
SPCN 25116.01656
Class Report Envelope
SPCN 25116.02822 (Pack of 10)
Offering Envelopes
SPCN 25116.02156 (Pack of 50)
Teacher Certificate
SPCN 25116.02180 (Pack of 10)
VBS Registration/Attendance Cards
SPCN 25116.02199
Visitor's Registration Slip
SPCN 25116.02849

STICKERS
Hot-Air Balloon Stickers
UPC 607135.000822
Bible Characters Stickers
UPC 607135.000839
Alpine Wildlife Stickers
SPCN 25116.01664
Frontier Life Stickers
SPCN 25116.04760
High Country Plants & Flowers Stickers
SPCN 25116.01672
Pioneer Trappin's Stickers
SPCN 25116.04744

Prairie Animals Stickers
SPCN 25116.04752
Christian Symbols Stickers
SPCN 25116.04779
Beach Toys Stickers
SPCN 25116.05767
Cars and Trucks Stickers
SPCN 25116.07328
City Animals Stickers
SPCN 25116.07344
Friendly Neighbors Stickers
SPCN 25116.07336

Available through your local Christian Supplier Gospel Light